A MILD CASE OF DEAD

The unseen toll of America's obsession with health, fitness and weight loss

by

Dave Young

Copyright © 2022 | Dave Young Communications, Inc.

All rights reserved.

ISBN: 0-9987662-0-8

ISBN 13: 978-0-9987662-0-1

CONTENTS

Introduction — *i*

ONE
How. Are. You. — *1*

TWO
Phantom:Life — *31*

THREE
Phantom:Health — *49*

FOUR
Phantom:Fitness — *65*

FIVE
Phantom:Diet/Weight Loss — *109*

SIX
For Scientists Only — *127*

SEVEN
Where's My Trophy? — *141*

EIGHT
Alive Instead — *159*

NINE
A Mild Case of Dead — *169*

TEN
A Bigger Life — *185*

Introduction

I love discovering comedians who make me laugh till I hurt. For my money, Dmitri Martin checks all the boxes. Watching a video clip of his recently, I heard this: "Someone said to me once that he was really good at checkers. I said, 'Wow, you must not be good at very many things'."

At first, that struck me as merely funny. I say "merely" because later I also realized that this quip was a comedian's way of saying something that I had been wanting to write a book about since my days as a health club owner and athletic coach. This is that book, and here is a more direct—but waaay less funny—way to say it:

The natural world punishes the specialist and rewards the generalist.

It's easy to miss this fact of life when messages coming from so many places would have us believe the opposite. The messages most of us hear in modern life glorify specialists (masters of just about anything) and characterize generalists as uninspired or lazy or both.

Whatever the choice of a specialty—checkers, a spot on the Forbes List, or a spot in the Tour De France—the world can and does turn a blind eye to glaring chinks in a person's character if they are masters of something.

Why do humans glorify specialization when nature does not? There is a part of each of us that lives in defiance of the natural world and the human spirit. That part of us is our capacity for logic and its byproduct, the human ego. To our capacity for logic winning the game of recognition is the bottom line of life when in fact it is only the bottom line of the ego.

While mastery of some discipline may give you a free pass from the societal rules that govern most of us, it comes at a steep price to the quality of your life. Philosophers through the ages have alluded to this through quotes like this one from the 14th century: "A jack of all trades is a master of none, but oftentimes better than a master of one."

All we need to see the value of generalization is to be a casual observer of life as it is lived and has always been lived. Early life for our species demanded that our ancestors be generalists. They had only themselves to rely on for all matters of life. There were no experts or authorities or for-hire consultants to help us overcome the multifaceted challenge of survival in a natural environment. Our ancestors' task was creating a great life for themselves and doing all that implies. They simply didn't have the luxury of specializing, and it's easy to see that specialization would have been catastrophic to survival.

Still, it was a great life. If it had not been, our species would have died out long ago. Our survival is a strong clue that nature rewards the generalist and punishes the specialist. We also know that our species has not changed much since its earliest days. This understanding still exists in us at the level of instinct and perhaps at an even deeper level that we have yet to learn much about. But the evidence of its existence is all around us to this day.

What this history teaches is that specialization—regardless of the type, perception, or promise—has no connection to our satisfaction with life. However, it does produce a feeling in us that mimics that satisfaction. The human ego has its own design for us, and we are often fooled into thinking the satisfaction derived from being a master of something represents the quality of our lives. In reality, it is only the quality of our ego.

Where else does this misunderstanding, along with so many others, show up in our lives? One area is the abnormal attention so many of us give to the notions of health, fitness, and weight loss strategies. Would it surprise you to learn that these are among the very specialties that nature discourages? They are pursued by those struggling to find some better experience of life, but the only experience they can produce is just different, not better. The struggle doesn't end there.

What motivates all personal development, no matter the name it has or the form it takes, is a better experience of life. This pursuit also creates a drive for wealth, power, and fame. By now, though, most of us would outwardly admit those achievements are ego-driven, and provide no guarantee of this greater experience. Those already living a satisfied life have no need for any of them. But have we had that same realization about the goals of health, fitness, and weight loss? How have these matters so far escaped the reality check of this connection?

Any discussion about those subjects that doesn't include a presumption of nobility has the feel of heresy. But sometimes what we consider heresy says more about our cultural investment in something than the value of it. Speaking about health as a distraction from life lies far outside the beliefs sanctioned by society. That's why a willingness to drop the need for society's approval is a prerequisite for a more objective and honest understanding of these subjects. People will look at you funny.

I want to share with you my observations from the many years I spent in the field of health, nutrition, and fitness coaching as well as the results of that work in the lives of my clients. The overriding theme of everything I learned in that time was the wisdom of honoring life ahead of fitness routines and dietary rules. Too many people, perhaps even you, are unaware that these are not the same thing but, in fact, are mutually exclusive goals.

I was never a traditional fitness coach. From the beginning I disliked that common fitness practices and programs seemed to care little for the person inside of the client. Much of my attitude then and now is best expressed by this well-known Deepak Chopra quote:

"Body and mind are not separate. They should be considered as one thing, and inextricable."

As many already know, traditional fitness training is made up of numerous specialty practices and disciplines that—despite being radically different from one another—all fly under the banner of "fitness." They cover the spectrum from aerobics to weight training and everything in between. Whatever specific benefits the client is looking for, there is a specialty that claims to provide it. And most are conducted in purpose-built facilities that claim to offer the perfect environment for that program.

Whatever else they may accomplish, these specialty programs are designed to productize fitness first. The intent of productization is to make the goal inseparable from the provider. Products, by nature, are mass-appeal constructs. Economies of scale are the quickest, and sometimes the only, road to profits. But "mass appeal" also means that products are less about you, and more about some faceless universal customer. In essence, this is the distinction between fitness and life: Fitness is a universal truth, life is a personal truth.

It's not enough to just say you agree with a quote. Real agreement is found when the principle forms a basis for your life choices. What I saw in the fitness world was an intent to separate the mind and the body for the sake of convenience, productization, and, ultimately, profit. So, I made it my mission to put the "personal" back into fitness by creating programs that produce more vital people rather than just more attractive, or even better performing, bodies.

The problem with my plan to mingle life enhancement strategies with traditional fitness was that the specialties were dominating the process. The more limited and specific the activity, the more mastery demands repetition and details, leaving little to no opening for addressing the greater life of my clients.

That's when it dawned on me that traditional fitness specialties and life-enhancement strategies were distinct processes with mutually exclusive goals. One was the universal truth of common goals, the other was the personal truth of individual goals. That realization led me to the discovery that this same principle shows up elsewhere in the realms of self-care: all have become logical interpretations of the process through productization. Logic is what drives our attraction to specialization by answering personal questions with universal answers.

Health-as-life in all its forms is an entirely personal matter, but logical humans tend to look for universal strategies. These strategies tend to invite debate rather than provide answers. Whereas, personal truths are instantly recognizable, but only by the individual wanting to know.

All this leaves individuals with results that are different in both kind and degree when the process is in the form of a product than when it is in the form of an experience. The experiential version is always personal, while the productized version is always common and reproducible.

But putting your faith in someone else's list about important choices for life is a form of outsourcing the experience of it; a ridiculous notion at best. It's a little like winning the lottery and then allowing someone else to spend the money to ensure that it was spent "correctly." Far more satisfying results are found in creating your own plan than consulting an expert about their's.

It can be profoundly unsettling to find oneself at odds with something as deeply ingrained in the world as the nobility of health or even—and perhaps especially—an obsessive pursuit of it. It's a little like questioning our collective belief in gravity. But all real epiphanies about life begin just that way: a questioning from somewhere deep inside, regardless of how it conflicts with the world view. Are you up for a little of the same questioning for yourself?

The agenda of profits and a general lack of integrity in our language has resulted in the hijacking of the words available to us to describe the potential for human life. This manipulation has to do with maximizing the ability to make money from health rather than producing thriving lives. There are few in modern times who are willing to challenge popular thinking on these subjects, so this is a lonely road for those who do.

This will be your challenge as well. But remember always that your humanity lies deeper than observable qualities; it is not easily identified or talked about. Seeking to satisfy logical constructs is far easier, but only serves to satisfy others and deny yourself.

I'll be speaking more about some of the valuable lessons I learned as a coach and gym owner, including my work with professional athletes, as we go along. But despite my clients' physical accomplishments, many were among the most troubled people I knew. Not troubled in any overt way—they were not, by and large, lawbreakers or violent, but were just more anxious and unsettled in life.

Being troubled in this way is not a failing, just the result of a misunderstanding about life. But it is intensified and chronic unless we choose to address it rather than the symptoms of it. The greatest obstacle is denial. Meanwhile it does show up in some very predictable ways. One of those ways is the demand for structure and reason, even when structure and reason defeat the goal.

The time and energy required to achieve any degree of physical specialization necessarily detracts from the focus someone must devote to the internal issues of life. This is a classic case of structure over experience as a value. And that punishment I mentioned earlier is an escalation of anxiousness and confusion. Appearance, or even physical performance, is not a solution for a life still seeking its peace. Yet, that is how they are used.

The reason a specialized life is an unfulfilled life is not only that it demands an unnatural commitment of time and energy focused on a specific skill or quality, it also puts us squarely in a mindset that is the very cause of our dissatisfaction. It satisfies logic but never experience, so a pursuit of physical excellence may be the very cause of our discomfort instead of the solution to it.

There is an obvious rationale behind the notions of health,

diet, and fitness, but how they are practiced reveals that they are entirely self-centered pursuits that seek mostly recognition and envy in others. This is a sign of deeper trouble that leads to an equally obvious neglect of those deeper aspects of life.

A specialist may indeed contribute something beautiful to the world, but that contribution alone is not the subject here. We are here to talk about being remarkably satisfied with our lives, which is always the goal of humanity. When ultimate satisfaction with life is the goal, the inevitable result is not only the peace and creative energy of our design, but also our undeniable ability to contribute to the world around us. The opposite is not true.

A human can never be observed as being good at life, when good is only a personal experience. And our egos—a subset of logic—wants to be observed as being good at something. Those who pursue a physical specialty seeking recognition instead of experience will always seek to make their efforts known, acknowledged, supported, and envied by others by announcing their accomplishments proudly and broadly. Any use of logic to improve our quality of life through specialization makes sense only when people are around to acknowledge the effort. Even being good at checkers is, apparently, worth mentioning.

Realize that mastery of the physical realm is a creation of modern life, not a virtue of our humanity. Your sense of logic will try to convince you that the pursuit of a specialty such as fitness (and all its derivatives), a regimented diet, or weight loss is a noble one for reasons other than the recognition it brings, but that is almost never true. The very fact that these are specialties at all is evidence of that.

The primary message of this book is this: Health, as it is currently practiced and talked about, is not a life-affirming quality but rather a productization of life. The value of this message is in the simple acknowledgment of that fact, not in any specific actions. Whatever changes that acknowledgment brings about in your life is entirely up to you, and any attempt by me to dictate those changes would be a contradiction of the secondary message of this book: You already know what to do and you always have.

Besides the recognition specialties bring, being good at checkers or health or fitness or food choices or any number of other specialties guarantees you no other quality of life but that. Others may acknowledge that you're good at something, but that is never a comment about the quality of your experience, nor should it be confused with achievement.

No one else is ever in the position to judge or instruct you on the quality of your life. That is a matter for personal discovery only. But living as a fulfilled human is a far greater prize than fitting into a smaller size of clothing. And, a failure to pursue the greater end will always result in what I call "a mild case of dead." Or, in some of us, a more severe and persistent case.

It's revealing to consider books about success, personal development, and self-help in the same way that you would also think of books about dominating the game of checkers. Would the net result of the time and energy it took to master the various specialties taught in those books actually be a more satisfying life or just another skill? Do all of the self-help, by-the-numbers plans really have more in common with mastering the game of checkers than they do with mastering the quality of your life?

If we fail to recognize why we're here, it is all too easy to become convinced that we can gain satisfaction in life by being great at checkers or health or fitness or weight loss or Instagram. This is especially easy if many other people—checkers coaches and Instagram followers, for instance—are also convinced and standing by to acknowledge that mastery. Their approval is based on the misunderstanding that mastery in any of those things equates to being good at life.

As you can see, reading this book will require some serious soul-searching and courage along with a willingness to abandon some long-held beliefs about the value of all life, starting with your own. Following other people's plans and wanting to emulate their enviable accomplishments just makes you a copy of them. Instead, I'm here to talk about your uniqueness as an individual and your potential for changing your experience, and the world, as no one else can.

A Mild Case of Dead is about taking deeply personal responsibility for the general work of life instead of the outsourcing so common with specialization. It is not for the faint of heart or those easily distracted from the real job of creating a great life. But if you are not satisfied with measuring your life by numbers rather than experiences, this book is for you.

The book is about the many different games we attempt to master, including Dmitri's checkers, but that can also masquerade as life itself. No matter how much recognition they bring, they are also barriers to the better internal life for which we were designed. These games are nothing more than logical versions of living, which is no life at all.

Specifically, this book is about the games of health and its many offshoots such as weight loss, bodybuilding, fitness, and even competitive athletics. These were specialties of mine but ones I no longer consider noble. I have come to know them as symptoms of, and contributors to, a crisis of spirit. But they are only symptoms of the dysfunctional and dehumanized culture in which we find ourselves.

Just as with the mastery of skill or appearances, the only possible outcome of chasing the phantom goals of health, diet, and fitness is that you will never arrive (more on that statement later). Yet, there is such a thing as *your life*, and that life could and would be better by far today if you never made any of those specialties a thing to master. The authentic form of those disciplines—such that they contribute to your experience—will always occur naturally as a byproduct of a life well lived.

Life is a value and goal unto itself. Health, dietary regimens, and fitness are just a few of modern life's attractive distractions from it; they are phantom goals that can promise only a life as defined by others but are ultimately corrupters of the one defined by you. They result in a condition aptly named *A Mild Case of Dead*.

They are checkers by another name.

ONE

How. Are. You.

Key Message:
Far too many lives are suffering from simple neglect. Suffering lives are nonetheless full of data and scientific analysis and "living right."

I am often asked if I've read a particular book on personal development that goes by a title such as The 7 Steps to [This] or The 5 Habits of [That]. The truth is that I generally avoid reading books with a number in the title. To suggest a personally successful life can be found in numbers, programs, or formulas strikes me as missing the point of life. If you are searching for a "formula for success"—especially if "success" for you is just feeling better—I'd like you to know that formula does not exist. In the pages to come, you'll learn why that is fantastic news.

Regardless, you're no doubt aware of how many of these by-the-numbers books consistently end up on best-seller lists and make plenty of money for their publishers and authors. They do so because they appeal to a part of us that operates on theory, data, numbers, and other logical constructs. All quantification is nothing more than theories about life. Contrast that with another part of each of us: the one that honors the actual and current experience of our lives. Is that experience a good one or less so? That is the question health is supposed to answer.

Theories about life appeal to our capacity for reason, certainty, realism, and other noble-sounding notions. In other words, there's a baked-in part of us that measures life by its "correctness" rather than the quality of the experience. That part is the logical brain. When unchecked by the subtler influences of our humanity, the logical workings of the brain will permeate every area of our lives, down to and including even the reason we are here.

The simplest way to understand these conflicting views of life is to answer one simple question: "How are you?" It's no accident that it is one of the most common queries in all the world because it is evidence that we are all striving to know each other better through our individual experiences. But the way we treat that question shows that we don't really know ourselves at all.

Far too many of us don't want to think about, let alone talk about, how we are. How we are occurs to many of us as a distraction from the job of doing life correctly; we can't find any relevance for it in our current pursuit of the way life should be lived. But when we hide our true nature from the world, we also end up hiding it from ourselves.

Most of us will treat the question as a request for data or for other information about our lives. Or we may consider it an invitation to compare our lives to the prevailing theory about what a life should be. So, we often answer with facts and figures and circumstances rather than an explanation of how those things are affecting us.

But "how are you?" is not a request for data. It is a request to connect on the level of experience, which is the only real quality of any life. You won't ever connect with another person through data, theories, numbers, or formulas. It is only by an experience of life that you uncover a deeper part of other people and they, you. When only information is exchanged, it is not unlike meeting with your accountant when you were hoping to see a Broadway play. Isn't it also true that, when you're doing the asking, you're just a bit disappointed when you get only data-driven information as a response?

An honest and experience-based answer to that question is an important link to some critical awareness about life. It's so important, in fact, that I'll be using the rest of these pages to explain why you should never lose touch with how you are to the point of answering that question reflexively or with a rehearsed response.

Let's realize too that the question is often asked by those who don't really want to know nor expect to hear how you are. But here's the worst part: most of us don't even know the real answer anyway, and we've long since forgotten how to know. We may have forgotten that there's any benefit to knowing. So we take the question in the spirit it was asked, and we lie. We lie to those who ask, and just as often, we lie to ourselves.

What if someone really—I mean, really!—wants to know how you are. You can always provide an honest answer to that question, and it's likely far different from the polite one you routinely offer up. Consider for just a moment that being acutely aware of how your life is going at this moment is a pretty great exercise to engage in. Considering all the aforementioned fakery, though, it's entirely possible that you haven't engaged in that process in a very long time. And perhaps you have forgotten how to answer the question honestly.

Do most of us even know that life is supposed to be a magical experience, not merely a logically correct one? Many will settle for normal, believing that "surviving" is as good as it gets, as evidenced by a response of "fine" when we are asked how we are. This is mostly because we have lost touch with what life is supposed to be, how great we are designed to feel, and where, exactly, that greatness comes from.

How you are is the only reason you are motivated to change your diet or go to the gym. But that new diet and commitment to exercise never change the way you answer the question. We are generally numb to the experience of that, believing instead that if we are pain free and have some assurance that the basic necessities of life are available to us, life is as good as can be expected.

Feels Better, Is Better

So, where does the actual experience of your life matter, however it's going at the moment? Is a better quality of that experience important? Unlike with reason and correctness, in the experience of life, there are no absolutes. Being human is, instead, a fluid thing and always a matter of degree. It will be different tomorrow than it is today, and there are lesser and greater degrees of it.

The quality of your experience is known to you only and is never subject to any clinical or outside interpretation. It is known in the form of a felt sense, not numbers on a medical chart, the bathroom scale, plates on a barbell, miles run, expert opinion, or even a financial statement. What all of those measures have in common is that they are customary ways to avoid the question of whether we are actually experiencing a better life. If not, how do we get there?

Even though a generalized approach to life still requires

specific actions on our part, those actions will rarely if ever be referred to by a name like health, fitness, or proper diet. There is never a need to discuss them in general conversation, just as we wouldn't necessarily be compelled to debate the scientific merits of brushing our teeth or wearing clean clothes. They are, instead, just some of the many acts we engage in as a way of honoring our lives. How much do we really need to know about brushing our teeth or wearing clean clothes? And what motivates those simple acts?

The answer to those questions is the experiential and creative approach to health, fitness, and diet, which is to say you do them, but you already know what you need to know. Those actions are never a subject for debate or much scientific study.

Plus, it would be hard to imagine that you consider those acts to require much "will power" or "self-discipline" to maintain. There are no buildings full of toothbrushes and spare clothes that you need to visit every day to practice the latest techniques so that you are appropriately skilled at those acts. Finally, there are no YouTube channels or subject matter experts or coaches offering masterclasses to pay for.

I'm suggesting just what you think I'm suggesting: The maintenance of your body so that it supports what is really important about your life requires no more of your knowledge and attention than brushing your teeth and wearing clean clothes. I suppose you could always make health more important and mysterious if you want to, just as you could getting your teeth clean, but why? What would that contribute to anything important about being a human alive? And what other experiences and rewards of life are you ignoring while you're ensuring you have the very cleanest clothes on the block? That is when clean clothes become your own version of a specialty.

New Idea, New Word

My word for a bigger picture of life is Aliveness, meaning the whole of life and the generalized approach to fulfillment that reaches its full potential. It involves the stuff you must do as a simple honoring of life (like remaining vital and wearing clean clothes) to invite a better answer to the question "how are you?" and nothing more. In that sense, to enjoy a high level of Aliveness de facto means that you already are the only version of "healthy" that is necessary for that life. If there are to be bodily changes in your future, they will arrive effortlessly and without the need for experts, science, or formulas.

Too many of us treat life as something that must be controlled and managed instead of something to be honored and experienced for its own sake. This approach is the result of a logical view of the world that promotes a disassociated form of life in which everything but logic's own sense of self (the ego) is an enemy to be managed and controlled.

Another way to say it is that we *control and manage* because we're not happy with who we already are. We may also be unhappy with things like vitality and body fat, but those things are not *who we are*. They are merely circumstances and misunderstandings about life and our place in it.

The biggest misunderstanding of all is equating circumstances like physical weakness and excess body fat with being a flawed and unacceptable human. This perception is what leads to adopting unnatural and obsessive fitness and health practices and products in a desperate attempt to eliminate any observable markers of our perceived flaws to the outside world.

In truth, these physical issues are only current circumstances and the result of how we have chosen to spend our time—not *who we are*, or even *how we are*. That distinction changes everything about how you approach getting back on track in a physical sense.

The way we have chosen to spend our time is not a flaw and is not unacceptable, and it needs no justification or endorsement from anyone. In fact, it likely satisfied other needs and desires in your life of which others are completely unaware. You have always been in complete control of that, and you will continue to be in the future.

So, chronically poor results like (lifestyle-induced) physical degeneration of all types are nothing more than the predictable results of how we have spent our time. But if we choose to see it as a personal failing it will produce a form of desperation that drives us to unnatural remedies rather than the ones we already know.

I saw this desperation first-hand time after time, year after year, in the eyes of new clients who would come for a consultation or some initial coaching sessions. It was easy to spot that much of their self-image was tied to achieving a physical state based on cosmetic or performance values—or some other combination of observable results.

But that is a role that our physical design was never meant to play, and whatever can be created in the gym or with a regimented diet will always be transitory. Even the recognition they bring is transitory. Yet, your self-image should never be based on something transitory. It can be something of your own design and making, and something that no one can ever take from you.

When you can separate *who you are* and *how you are* from

your current results, you realize that the solution is to change the meaning you assign to those results. When it is only a circumstance and not *who you are*, it will change the way you conduct your entire life. Your "entire life" means your beliefs, your attitudes, and your lifestyle in total—the whole 24/7 of it, not just your gym hours or your pill count or the "don't eat that" parts of it.

What I'm suggesting here is that being happy with who you already are, and despite your current circumstances, is pretty good advice not only for your physical state, but for so many aspects of life.

"How are you?" is similar to "what do you want?" Most of us struggle equally with both questions because the answers come from the same place and are equally unjustifiable and unreasonable according to the rules of logic.

Logic dictates that we demand obedience and adherence to rules as the first requirement of acceptance—for our dogs, our children, and our bodies—instead of simply honoring the life in them. We have come to believe that our own bodies are the enemy of our lives and must be made to obey and conform to some artificial standard that is entirely foreign to it but sanctioned as "correct" by others. Eventually, all that managing and controlling takes the form of beating our bodies into submission with structured workouts and rigid diets.

Think for a moment about the conversations you hear all around you. This includes advertising, "news" articles, success advice, self-help books, health club chatter, etc. Health, fitness, diets, and wealth (a.k.a., financial security) are among the most prominent topics of discussion, and in that discussion these concepts are mostly treated as if they were life itself. At the very least, to be accomplished in any of those ways is considered a mark of "character" and achievement. Even the most basic of accomplishments in the physical realm—weight loss—is headline news! And the "news" is about either the people who have produced some observable change, or breakthroughs that will make that change easier in those who haven't.

That is the very reason that so many people seek it out as a focus of their effort and bestow upon it a level of reverence and importance that it simply does not deserve. And those who make money from this industry are happy to play along, and cash the checks. I did. Not only does it contribute surprisingly little to the quality of our actual lives, the little that it does contribute can be easily produced with no outside assistance at all.

More importantly, there is no "new information" under the sun. In the realm of this thing we call fitness, there never was any new information, only what can create the image of it without the substance of it. In other words, what passes for new knowledge is just strategies for producing the same results without having to actually deny yourself life's many pleasures. Everything else you need to know is part of the internal wisdom of every individual that they can easily deduce for themselves.

Wanna be healthy and fit in every way that matters? Care about your life. Then, care about your life more. This "caring" is not an act of will, something that requires motivation, discipline, or something else to add to your to-do list. The path to caring about your life is the same as the path to your highest potential; that is, to first become aware of what you're doing instead. What you're doing instead is occupying your mind to an extent that you have nothing left with which to be aware of your actual life.

Consider this alternative to the current thinking about

health and fitness: It's harder to be limited by the state of your body (unhealthy) than it is to be supported by that state (healthy). And those of us experiencing limitation based on the condition of our bodies know that we are not idle bystanders of the process that got us there.

We actively participated in the decline of our physical wellbeing. We participated by making some other aspect of life the focus of our time. There is no failing in that, only the recognition that there was some perceived benefit to you for that choice that requires no justification. Correction, maybe. But there is no mystery here. Your physical state is always a reflection of how you have spent your time.

Wouldn't it make sense to begin the journey of bodily improvement (what most of us know of as the pursuit of health) by understanding more about the process that created the decline? Instead, most of us approach this process by going to the gym where all that happens is an attempt to correct the damage (because that's all we can really do with exercise). That is a cycle doomed to repeat.

Please recognize that modern-day exercise is an entirely human-made construct that is just a convenient and sometimes money-making guess about the cause and effect of physical decline. If that doesn't immediately resonate with you never fear because I have a whole chapter on this subject coming that will explain it in much greater detail.

You Are the Expert

The very first thing to know about the maintenance of your body is this: Relax! I don't mean sit on the couch all day watching TV, but you know that already. Rather, relax on the inside. The idea is to release the grip that guilt and confusion has on you and stop forcing your body into weird adaptations for the sake of appearances or even performance. Those things never constitute a purpose in life or a quality experience. Forgetting that fact is the source of much internal suffering and mental illness in the world.

Whatever else you may want to call a notion of health that is distinct from other aspects of your life, it is never a mandate for achieving your full potential as a human. It is not so much the idea of health that I object to; rather, it is the seriousness and reverence for the theory that is held by so many. This overblown nobility places it squarely in the realm of a distraction from life, not a requirement for the things we all want from life.

The solution we seek is never found in information, will power, formulas, plans, routines, "steps for success," motivation, or most of what is referred to as effort and discipline. Those are notions that sound like they *should* be true, and make motivational speakers lots of money, but don't add a wit to your life. A better experience is served by the intent to simply honor your life in every way that enhances it. That experience is its own reward.

As I coached my clients on the various aspects of health and fitness, I found myself having to bring up some decidedly common-sense details like, "Don't eat stuff that is handed to you through a small sliding window while you sit in your car."

These clients, by the way, were largely financially successful and otherwise intelligent folks, so it was hard for me to understand how these rudimentary choices could be new to them. Since this was clearly not a matter of intelligence, what else was going on that had obscured the obviousness of these choices?

I eventually realized that these otherwise bright people had been systematically schooled to believe that their own innate wisdom in matters of fitness and diet were untrustworthy and inferior to the advice of "experts" and other holders of certifications and diplomas, and marketing language. We were all being taught that we don't know enough to take care of ourselves. This perspective, of course, works out well for the bank accounts of those experts, but it is not true.

This schooling was taking place not only through the obvious agenda of marketing stuff for sale but also because it is these very same experts and certificate holders who are authoring the most widely featured articles and books on these subjects. It seems unlikely that they would be willing to say you don't need what that honorific attached to their names gives them a platform to teach.

Life: An Inside Job

A generalized approach to life is one that focuses on internal matters of innate wisdom equally with the external ones. "External" is the stuff of performance, body weight, and cosmetics and the recognition we receive for them. It includes all the purely physical pursuits that contribute little to our internal wellbeing. It's easy to see how most of what we know of as health and fitness falls into that category.

By contrast, "internal" is the stuff that only you know and that only you will ever feel; it is *how you are*. And that enhances your life in ways that cannot be realized by any other means. You pursue internal matters when no one else is looking and when you don't care if anyone is. Satisfaction would be one word for it. This feeling is often also referred to (wrongly, I believe) as mental or emotional health.

Depression is an example of a poor internal experience. It's easy to see that no one else can truly understand the source or experience of your depression. Nor will anyone else validate what seems to you to be the unassailable truth causing your depression. In the same way, you will never receive recognition or be envied for the opposite of depression: a great experience of life. It is just for you to experience. For those reliant on logic for their guidance, this will be a deal breaker; no matter how bad they currently feel.

Most people, I believe, would acknowledge the folly of encouraging a depressed person to hit the gym five days a week without first dealing with the cause of the depression. It is obvious that whatever results could be realized by that exercise would be only temporary and, sooner or later, sabotaged by the source of the depression.

And what if depression were simply a matter of degree and the majority of us were unknowingly suffering from it? Then, what if far too many of us were engaged in the artificial act of modern-day health practices in the hopes of curing our dissatisfaction with life? Would you not view that as a logical but flawed strategy? I would like to suggest that this is closer to the truth of it in modern times.

That observation brings us back to the concept of Aliveness. Essentially, Aliveness is the experiential answer to the question "how are you?" It is the sum total of everything that determines the quality of your life at this moment. Any attempt to parse your life into smaller pieces and parts, clinical values, situations and conflicts, physical and mental, will degrade the level of Aliveness you enjoy. Think of it as a currency measured by the degree of satisfaction.

The opposite of Aliveness is a logical interpretation of life that seeks correctness and absolutes. Logic is what leads us to seek out experts and coaches and fitness trainers and practitioners and clinicians of all kinds to analyze our numbers and prop us up when the numbers drop too low (or rise too high).

Any attempt to reduce life to something quantifiable is ultimately destructive to the experience of that life. Considering how much measuring we actually do, this realization should come as a bit of a shock. Could it be that the internal suffering so many of us experience is a direct result of that measuring? Could it be that honoring numbers as the measure of life only means we doom ourselves to failure?

There is nothing in the external world of numbers and recognition that deserves respect on the level of nobility. "Nobility" is that unquestioning reverence for the value of something to the point that the worth of it exceeds your own worth. If you automatically accept the fact that you don't know enough to take the proper care of your body, that is a sure sign that you've given it a degree of nobility that it doesn't deserve, and you will not benefit from that designation in any significant way. That perception is likely the result of assuming that the societal paradigm on those subjects is somehow crucial to life, when in fact it is only a theory at best and a sales pitch at worst.

The Aliveness approach to life is to simply observe your own personal experience of it and, without judgment, make adjustments to improve it. If you're quantifying your life in any way—steps per day, miles per week, maximum load lifted, pounds lost (or gained), calories consumed, cholesterol levels, for example—you are measuring instead of experiencing.

Measuring is a logical construct and, as such, relies on judgment to assess the numbers: This number is good, that number is bad. Observing is nonjudgmental—the only goal is to make it more enjoyable in ways that only you can. A personal and private monitoring of your ongoing experience will cause you to respond with internal wisdom rather than pills or formulas or diets when conditions begin to affect your experience.

The Productization of Life

By now, I'm sure you're beginning to see those ideas such as health, fitness, sports performance, and weight loss are all logical constructs. They are meaningless unless they are being measured, compared, judged, bragged about, worried over, and debated. This is not the stuff of a satisfied life; this is the stuff of the brain and its pursuit of recognition through correctness. All those values are, at best, a distraction from the real goal of a fulfilled life. At worst, they are corrupters of our humanity and relationships. Who remembers who came in second, no matter how much effort or sacrifice it took to get there?

All by itself, and apart from any measure of health and fitness, life is a fantastic experience. Experience needs to be the new benchmark, but this value is never an absolute, and therefore of no interest to our egos. Is it possible to be too fantastic? If you can't say with conviction and authority that your life is a fantastic experience, the problem is not in your health, weight, or fitness, but in your understanding of life.

The majority of the people who populated my gym and almost every gym I've spent time in would not readily say they were there to achieve a greater experience of life. Make no mistake—a better experience of life is what everyone wants, but that quality has no name, is not quantifiable, and is only indirectly observable by others. Therefore, it is not talked about or acknowledged as a thing or as having a source. Instead, we are aware only of the logical and observable version of a better experience: fitness and health.

Logic does not comprehend, nor will it condone or support in any way, the human spirit. Instead, it seeks solutions in the physical, tangible, external aspects of life. This approach serves the goal of survival well because external forces are the only threats to our existence. They show up as pressures like wanting to be better than others at something, thus increasing the draw of specialization. But our ability to enjoy any external quality of life can never exceed our ability to enjoy the internal one.

Despite my mother's many other qualities, she was not the most enlightened soul on the planet, to put it mildly. She was very much stuck in a logical interpretation of life. After my sister returned from a recent trip to a country not known for its wealth or innovation, she nevertheless commented on how happy the people seemed to be. My mother quite matter-of-factly replied, "What good is happiness if you haven't got any money?" Your own capacity for logic might suggest that was a perfectly rational position. But is it a human position? The two are not the same thing.

That simple shift in personal reality likely explains so much of the difference in our thinking that can result in either real satisfaction or constant striving and struggle. If my mother held the logical viewpoint, the purely experiential version would be that happiness is the only goal worth pursuing, for the simple reason that money isn't ever an experience in and of itself. It is merely a symbol agreed upon by the world as representing something valuable. Is that also true of health, fitness, and diet?

Without a standard for the qualities known as fitness, health, and food choices, it should be silly to pursue them. After all, there is just no way to know how far we've come or when we've arrived other than being more disciplined than others. This one and only benchmark, regardless of the personal experience of it, is the modern version of health. We act as if we have completely forgotten that health is always and only an experience.

How many modern-day gym goers would show up every day in pursuit of this thing called fitness if the gym were otherwise empty or the rest of the world were blind? This fear of invisibility is precisely what is behind the question of "motivation" so many struggle with in their desire to be more consistent exercisers. And, why the modern qualities referred to as fitness and health are measured by their ability to be observable and worthy of recognition by others; that is the standard for success that humans will always adopt in the absence of any experiential value.

I have encountered very few people who were truly motivated by anything other than that recognition. When our own internal experience is poor, we're still not convinced there is anything abnormal about that. After all, "normal" is relative only to our own experience, so we seek the opinion of others as a way to know that we're considered a part of the normal world. But how absurd is it to ask someone else if we are happy?

Fitness, as it is practiced these days, whether the stated goal is performance or cosmetics, fails to produce real contributions to a person's internal life. What accompanies the recognition and envy is always a corresponding decline in experiential satisfaction, apart from the ego boost.

Don't get me wrong, ego boost is a real thing, and it can act as a reasonable substitute for actual happiness. But the key word there is "reasonable." True life satisfaction is never judged by its reasonableness or justified through acknowledgement by others.

In fact, even bodybuilders and fitness models—you know

the ones, from the covers of the fitness magazines—will tell you that sacrificing any hope of feeling good is considered to be the legitimate price for achieving that enviable appearance. This attraction to the superficial is not just a selfish act but also a destructive one.

Whatever gratification we find from recognition by others is nothing more than a satisfaction of logic. This is also what many call success; it may look like success, and others may also call it success, but it just doesn't *feel like* success. For those of us steeped in the logic of life, this is also what passes for happiness itself merely because satisfaction of the brain is the highest experience of which we are aware, not of which is possible.

Many people who showed up at my gym for coaching were often in some very dark places mentally and spiritually. Career dissatisfaction, alcohol or other addictions, dysfunctional relationships, imminent financial peril, depression, and other similar issues were impacting their overall quality of life. (You'd be surprised at what people are willing to share with a personal trainer that the rest of the world does not know about them.) These troubled folks were earnestly trying to transform their lives through this thing we were all calling fitness. But that's a little like marching off to war armed with only a scary story. You may cause your enemy to tremble a little, but the war will be lost.

Clearly, time in the gym was not the most urgent matter in their lives. Yet, there they were. I realized that they were there for one of two reasons: Either they were attempting to avoid making some tough decisions about life or they believed that time in the gym was somehow part of the solution. All fitness, health, and diet coaches must choose between their own integrity and allowing their clients some form of delusion in order to justify the money they charge and the work they do.

It is important to note that, in the pursuit of this thing called fitness, some relatively positive benefits can be had. But many of us consider those benefits to be something greater and more noble than they actually are, and we cling to those as if they represent all of life. Beyond that, the benefits that are available to us—and every living thing—when our full attention is on being experientially alive are exponentially greater.

Health Gone Bad

I rarely use the words "health", "fitness", "exercise", "workout", or "diet" anymore. But can you imagine owning a gym and trying to get through your day—or even the next hour—without using one of those words? Even if I could get some clients to see that there was a loftier goal for the work we were doing, most have been so conditioned to believe that aesthetics and recognition are the only goals worth working for that there was little interest in any other. And, that recognition is known today as "health", "fitness", "workout", and "weight loss", etc.

There are three primary intentions for physical activity: 1) quality-of-life and longevity, 2) athletic performance, and 3) aesthetics. The processes of effective training for each of those is entirely different, yet if profits are the only concern there is little need for fitness professionals to even mention this distinction.

Instead, serving the goal of aesthetics only while giving lip service to the other two will still guarantee the trainer 80 – 90% of the money they would have otherwise earned. And, that other 10 – 20% would cost far more than the additional revenue could justify. That extra money would be more than eaten up in education, equipment, and gym space.

So, there is little to no financial incentive to address anything but aesthetics and sport-specific performance in the typical health club environment. Nevertheless, I started my gym with the mission of changing that mindset, putting the experience of life at the top of the list in determining the type and degree of physical training, and as a way of charting success.

I quickly learned the hard financial lesson that this just didn't pay. Although clients initially nodded in agreement when I laid out this mission, time after time they would report they were quitting because they "weren't losing enough weight" or were failing to achieve some other artificial goal. Others were constantly checking themselves in the mirror for the shape and size of their muscles or the flatness of their stomachs. The messaging surrounding the health conversation now is so pervasively focused on appearances that it is hard for many people to conceive of much else.

Any work that includes the whole person instead of just their appearance is something that should never be subjected to the profit motive. Profits are counter-intentional to something as deeply personal as the quality of life. Profits are what spawned the obvious untruth, "the customer is always right." It would serve no purpose for the patients of a medical doctor or psychologist to claim to know more than the provider. But most would never make that claim because the medical community has been mostly successful at pushing back on letting the inmates run the prison.

Yet, in the search for profits by pandering to its customers, the fitness industry has allowed this customer-is-always-right message to prevail. Clients of health clubs have been conditioned to believe if they are paying money to attend, they have a right to call the shots. That was obviously one more well-established mindset that I was not going to change to any degree in the context of a gym.

And, make no mistake, the *context of a gym* is the root of the problem. Just the fact that there is a gym means that the customer has already been pandered to. The "gym" or "health club" wouldn't even exist if it wasn't for the expectation of convenience by clients; regardless of the contribution (or lack of) to their lives.

I had new clients tell me that they "don't want to get sweaty", and others who quit after the first session because the work made their muscles sore. To be fair, this was a minority of clients, but it meant that I couldn't help everyone that who claimed to want help. Those whose mindset about the process had been so corrupted by a profit-driven industry were unknowingly preventing themselves from improving their own lives.

Another interesting observation is the number of times soon-to-be brides, with only two weeks to the wedding, came to me requesting to lose 20+ pounds by the Big Day. Their entire reason for being there was the premise that there was something unacceptable about them that needed fixing, and nowhere in their markers for acceptability was the desire to experientially improve their lives.

(Sidebar: My main objection to rapid weight loss is the inescapable toll it takes on the quality of life in general, not to mention the physical toll on the body. Lots of fitness and health professionals will eagerly take on the job of helping someone achieve rapid weight loss, never mentioning or caring what effect it has on other aspects of life.

Those weight-loss strategies are well-known and fairly simple matters and lauded in fitness circles as fantastic scientific breakthroughs for their effects on body weight. And the fitness gurus that teach those methods are praised and sought after for their expertise. In those same laudatory reviews, the words "health" and "healthy" are stealthily sprinkled into the conversation to obfuscate the sad effects these practices have on the human experience.)

To those brides-to-be with their misguided requests for rapid and drastic weight loss, I often said, "In my professional opinion, the quickest and surest way to lose 20 pounds in two weeks is through the regular use of crack-cocaine. Any street-corner drug dealer can fix you up with a two-week supply of crack, and it will make you lose weight faster than I, or any fitness guru, can."

Despite the truth of it, I had to quickly add that the statement was not meant to be taken seriously (out of fear that it would be). It was, instead, just a way to make the point that any attempt at rapid weight loss is problematic in nearly every area of life. That is also the point about fitness in general as it is perceived and practiced by nearly all of us.

It probably won't come as a huge surprise to you that weight loss is the most popular goal for any dedication to physical activity. Bulging biceps and ripped abs come in a close second among men, while most women just want to be a certain clothing size. Whatever is said about the goals of fitness, if the results aren't visible and worthy of envy in others, most people will consider the work a waste of time. If they aren't acutely aware of life as an experience, it is easy to be sucked into that conversation without even realizing that there is another and much bigger prize available. "How are you?" Fantastic, thanks for asking.

It became also convenient for these otherwise intelligent

and sincere clients to convince themselves that the work they were doing in the gym was of greater importance than their experience of life. They had attached a sense of nobility and relevance to the work of (what is called) health and fitness. This relevance is universally supported in the societal paradigm but is just an illusion. Ironically, this attitude is often very destructive, depending on the style and aggressiveness of the practice. Perhaps you've noticed.

More times than I can count, I wanted to order clients out of the gym so they could pay attention to the crumbling fabric of their lives. Relative to that, what was happening in the gym seemed to me to be a trivial pursuit. But personal trainers don't make a lot of money by telling clients to go away and deal with more important matters, and by saying that their devotion to the work of fitness and health was either an avoidance strategy or a misunderstanding or both. Neither numbers or cosmetics care about the experience of life.

I can support people pursuing exceptional levels of physical appearance or performance, but not without an equal or greater commitment to the pursuit of exceptional levels of their own satisfaction with life. Without that, the results will be the very definition of superficial. Consider that any strategy for bettering life in the absence of internal work is also the driving force behind obsessional behavior, and there's certainly no shortage of that in the world of health, weight loss, and fitness.

In essence, too many of us have become numb to our own state of being in the moment, which is the most important awareness we can have for managing the quality of our lives. This numbness is the reason we have difficulty answering the question, "how are you?" Our awareness is fully consumed by the bright shiny objects of modern life, including information and competition, and other logical lessons we've learned about the "right" way to be. This is a numbness only of omission, not of commission. In other words, you can miss this vital role in life not by acting wrongly but simply by failing to act at all.

Eventually, I came to the unavoidable conclusion that the very concepts of health, fitness, and weight loss as we know them are artificial and substitute constructs that profit from people's fear of losing a competition called life. This is evidenced by the dread with which so many of us consider the need to exercise, which is a clue that this activity is not driven by a passion for the work. The only activities people perceive as vital are those that they are afraid to not do.

Here's a clue to what's important: If it isn't driven by passion, it's not life. Instead, it's merely a search for correctness and acceptance. Therefore, the entire health club/fitness industry would likely collapse quickly if it weren't for the people who use it as a substitute for the real work of their lives. Society provides plenty of support for that strategy because there's a lot of money to be made. Passion never sees effort as work.

There is no lasting and relevant change from the accomplishments of wealth, health, different food, or fitness in the absence of an authentic life. There can be numerical and cosmetic gains, but those are always theoretical, temporal, and logical rather than lasting and internally satisfying. That is the distinction between experience and logic, and between Aliveness and health.

When people have shut off access to their authentic selves, they turn to logical constructs such as coaches and experts and gurus and formulas and how-tos and numbers as a source of guidance and satisfaction with life. Logic gets a lot of things right, but a great experience of life is not one of them.

Inside-Out Health

Constructive advice about greater satisfaction in life will always value internal self-work above any of the relatively trivial matters of the purely physical. Self-work is among the most uncomfortable and frightening propositions most of us can imagine, and the initial response is to do almost anything to avoid it. Living correctly becomes an avoidance strategy; the avoidance of living authentically. That's the influence of logic on our thinking; a satisfied life is an inherently illogical life. Logic simply cannot comprehend the value of experience.

We find an opportunity for avoidance in logic because it always produces technically correct solutions and demands technically correct answers; things society applauds. But when it comes to the quality of a human life, there are no technically correct answers.

So the notion of a formula, 12-step programs, pills, potions, diets, or copy-cat how-tos is attractive mostly because it promises that we can achieve something that society considers to be success rather than what *we* as individuals consider to be success. Any success worth pursuing is yours and yours alone. No one else can ever tell you what a fulfilled life looks like, let alone how to achieve it.

The roots of logic are in the human brain. What all the distractions it produces have in common is that they are universally considered to be noble pursuits by society at large, and they result in some form of recognition by others. That promise satisfies our logical wants but not our experiential wants.

The goal of an experiential want is to simply feel good about ourselves and life, which shows up as things like freedom from fear, love, and laughter. That can always happen regardless of the opinion of others. It is always in the search for the logical want that we turn to experts, coaches, gurus, doctors, and "things for sale"—in this case, books, seminars, masterclasses, to name a few. These are all designed to pander to what logic demands: a correct answer.

As I mentioned earlier, I didn't enter into the field of health and fitness to help people have better bodies or even better health in the clinical sense; I wanted to help them have better lives. I learned two lessons from my interactions with my clients and from myself: 1) the logical need for recognition will win out over quality of life in the minds of most people because of the support it receives from society, and 2) a failure to value experience over all other goals will result in a troubled and dysfunctional life. At the heart of these failures is a reliance on logic (correctness, outside approval) for answers to the question, "How are you?"

That reliance explains why people often pursue serious fitness or athletic training in the first place; they want something that looks like, and is considered to be, success and that can be justified as correct and/or enviable. But they will know only the externally obvious trappings of that success and never the experience of it. That's because there simply isn't any.

For example, experiential fitness is far different from the logical fitness of competition, cosmetic values, and satisfaction of the need to be "doing something" with life. Experiential fitness is the capacity of the human body to support a maximum quality of life (as defined by the individual), including the activities that experience requires. That, and nothing more. No matter what it looks like.

Not surprisingly, that is still a level of physical capacity that exceeds the norm in modern society. The process of developing a purely constructive physical state is perceived as pointless drudgery to most because the results are rarely observable or worthy of envy.

Think of those people in your immediate circle who exercise in a gym or health club. How many of them are actually superior functionally? Try to look past the observable cues before you answer. Instead, try to identify those who you know to be superior performers in the broad sense; think survival in the natural world. You'll find the answer to be very few, if any.

So, this is what we're here to talk about: Life changes, not physical, not cosmetic, not even performance changes. Changes to the internal world instead of the external world. Changes that turn people's lives into a gift to everyone who comes in contact with them and to their own experience of it. Changes that produce the greatest improvements in life where it is lived. These are rarely discussed in the common conversation because they are unique to the individual and not available for judgment or debate. To the logical brain, that's boring and irrelevant. And these changes are never the result of anything called health, fitness, or diet.

A New Conversation

The new thinking is that "how you are" requires a hard and sincere, but nonjudgmental, observation of your current experience. To answer the question "how are you?" with a report on your medical condition or physical state is to put distance between you and the one who asked. Your experience may be affected by physical issues, but they are not the sum total of how you are.

Likewise, to base your experience of life on issues like health, fitness, or even diet is to base "how you are" on circumstances instead of experience. How you answer the question is all you need to know about your health. It's all you need to know about your fitness. It's all you need to know about your nutrition and your weight loss. It is *how you are.*

If you are done settling for the "correct" life of achieving six-pack abs or being a size zero and the "correct" answer to the question "how are you?", look now to the much larger notion of life where it is actually lived, where there is no longer anyone you wish to impress.

There are no "results from a recent scientific study" or "looking fit" that describe how you are. Far too many lives are suffering from simple neglect. Suffering lives are nonetheless full of data and scientific analysis and "living right." They just suffer from a lack of satisfaction and purpose.

To what degree does your life reflect that which simply brings you joy? Perhaps a joy of which no one else is even aware. Not money, not status, not the correct answer, not winning an argument, not the highest score, not the image in the mirror—just *how you are.* Those other goals are a distraction from the actual, present-moment experience of your life.

As you read this book, remember that references to "spirit" and "spiritual" are not about religion. In fact, I view organized religion as the logical interpretation of the message contained in this book. Logical interpretations are intriguing and usually satisfying on some level, but they are wholly unnecessary to the results we're trying to produce. Spirit is what inhabits your experience in the absence of any logical intent to be right.

All of us have the ability to change the world and live creative and fulfilled lives. That's how we are! The only reason any of us gives up on that promise is that we stop checking in with our real selves. That's the issue that needs resolving before any other. The logical version of "how am I?" is "how do other people perceive me? If others are satisfied that I am living a correct life, then so am I, regardless of how it all feels in the moment." This is the predominant belief around health, fitness, and weight loss.

What if, instead of living "correctly", we made purpose and fulfillment the measure of success? What if we made honoring our lives the path to fulfillment, instead of 10,000 steps on our wrist gadget? "Old" happens not to people with purpose but only to those who try to go on living without it. Purpose never sits on the couch and watches game shows. Purpose is always on its feet, creating something new.

Our current level of knowledge is substantial and completely adequate to living both better and longer lives. Purpose is what restores our drive to act on that knowledge rather than just debate it in our search for a better experience. We all have the ability to feel great at any moment and in any circumstance.

Does anyone choose "I lived correctly" as an epitaph? Why, then, is that the best thing many of us have to say about our lives while we are still among the living?

How. Are. You.

TWO
Phantom:Life

Key Message:
Where once the nature of life included all of the elements for a maximum experience of it, that process has become corrupted by an artificial version of it that we have labeled "new and improved."

To understand how concepts like health become corrupted in practice, we need to acknowledge how susceptible humans are to embracing "phantom" versions of important concepts. The official definition of phantom is "an appearance without substance; illusory."

The "substance" of life is always and only the experience of it. Nothing more. It becomes a phantom life when it is guided by the illusion of logical constructs that seek recognition rather than the quality of the experience. In other words, mistaking appearance and correctness for substance.

An important characteristic of experience is that it occurs in the body, not the brain. Since we must source our awareness from one or the other, we are incapable of having an experience unless we're listening to the body instead of the brain. Listening to the body is just another way of saying "experiencing."

Appearances, recognition, correctness, and analysis are all functions of the brain; logical functions.

We can say that health, fitness, and a regimented diet are about our health (the body), but our brain will quickly make them about appearances, recognition, and analysis as a way to do them correctly. This also serves the ego's purpose of shifting your awareness away from the body and onto the brain. It is only in being acutely aware of the brain/body distinction that we have any say in the matter.

Logical constructs begin with the premise that something is wrong that must be fixed, which results in a craving for information from outside sources, critical analysis, and a justifiable conclusion. This logical version of life is void of possibility and creation, but it is the only kind of life that the human brain can comprehend; that's what distinguishes thinking from experiencing.

Being abnormally reliant on logic as a way to view the world is the de facto standard for living in modern times. To be a fully alive human is not a simple matter, but the requirement for it is courage, not knowledge. This is the courage to be a different person, not the same person who just knows more. The challenge here is only in our inclination to perceive the version of ourselves that is most familiar as the only possible (or real) version.

The Hallmark of Life

According to logic, the opposite of simple is complex. The logical approach to life is to live it correctly. However, in the context of human life, the opposite of correct is not incorrect. If maximum Aliveness eludes us—mostly characterized by being unsettled and anxious in our experience—we think the problem is our lack of information. Yet, a better version of life will not result from more facts about it.

All these approaches suffer from the same failure to honor life by expecting it to be reasonable. The unreasonable approach is to realize that the opposite of both complex and correct is the essence of humor. More than any other quality, life can be described as funny, and humor is never defined by the process of reason or rationale. If you ever had to explain a joke to someone or had one explained to you, you know what I mean.

Humor isn't alone as an example of experience, but it is an easily relatable metaphor for life, as correctness is for logic. Logic can be satisfying in the same way that reconciling your bank account is satisfying, but it is a wholly different kind of satisfaction from an evening at a comedy club. Laughter is the momentary experience of being fully alive.

As you likely already know, the notions of health, fitness, and weight loss are never treated as funny. Most people treat them as deadly serious subjects for which only the correct and scientifically proven answer will do, which is a sure sign of a logical construct. Such constructs will always be corrupters of the experience of life, just as they are corrupters of humor.

The real purpose of logic in the context of being a human is to provide a path to safety in the face of imminent danger and threats to survival. In those situations, the continuance of life demands a correct answer. But in the absence of those threats, logic satisfies only itself, not the quality of human life. Logic operates in a human only because it can, because we allow it. It is a tool and a choice, not an edict.

This is where we take a closer look at how the phantom constructs of health, fitness, and weight loss can take over human life and rob it of possibility and creation, not to mention fun. The purpose is not to make a demon out of logic and its many constructs, but only to challenge the nobility that we have assigned to it wherever it shows up—as in health, fitness, and a technically correct diet—so that we can begin to see those constructs more honestly and in keeping with their actual contribution to our lives.

The Societal Paradigm

Humans have an abundant (some would say, excessive) capacity for logic. We are unique in that regard, but that capacity makes it tempting to inform our lives by correctness rather than the experience of them. Most of us will recognize our beliefs about health, fitness, and diet were acquired in just that way.

The phrase "societal paradigm" describes how we govern our behavior and improve our lives. It can be defined as the most prominent collection of messages on a given subject commonly circulating within a culture or society. It's a term meant to describe the aggregate source of an average person's information on seemingly important and often-discussed topics.

Societal paradigms show up in the strongest voices among friends and acquaintances; in the content of widely read books, news stories, and magazine articles; in broadcasts on radio and television; or in the digital realm of social media. Details about a societal paradigm are most of what's talked about in all of those forums in addition to simple everyday conversations. The totality of this chatter is what I will refer to from here on as the Conversation.

Societal paradigms are the subtext of the childhood tale The Emperor's New Clothes. In this story, the emperor's subjects had all been told that the emperor was sporting an impressive suit of new clothes, even though he was in fact naked. Because the information came from credible channels (the emperor's court), his subjects believed it more than they believed their own eyes.

In this context, believing your own eyes is the equivalent of believing your own experience, which includes your senses and your own innate wisdom. Plus, the more other people among the emperor's subjects acted and spoke as if the emperor were indeed wearing new clothes, the more each individual was willing to also act and speak as if it were true.

The Conversation is about the prevailing societal paradigm, even though our individual experience may suggest an entirely different reality. Think of it as a sort of mass delusion, a message that has broad acceptance as truth but is separate and apart from actual value to the individual.

We know in our hearts that only a fraction of what we hear through these various channels is both accurate and relevant (the test of usefulness), so we apply some personal test to the chatter to convince ourselves that we are accepting only the most credible information. Unfortunately, our personal test is a crude filter and is lacking in some important ways.

For example, both unestablished theories and outright deceptions that are repeated often enough usually sneak past our filter. These are accepted as truth for no other reason than the frequency with which we hear them and the number of sources from which they emanate. If a theory or deception can be placed consistently and in enough different places unchallenged, it is inevitably accepted as truth and becomes embedded in the Conversation. That is the story of The Emperor's New Clothes. And that is the story of health, fitness, and food choices.

Despite our attempt at truth-filtering (or perhaps because of it), this Conversation can and does promote strategies that appear reasonable but are actually destructive to the goal of life.

Our personal filter has also been corrupted by modern life. These new-day considerations include convenience, profits, image, money, or any number of other attractions that have been given society's stamp of approval as important but have nothing to do with truth or quality of life.

In today's world, these "truths" often originate in the marketing of things for sale. To understand marketing is to understand how to manipulate the societal paradigm and create a reflexive response for a private agenda; mostly, a profitable one. Never has this been more true than in this age of social media, when every message, no matter the source or usefulness, propagates because it originated with someone for whom followers have some affinity, not because of its truth in the life of the follower.

Logic OR Life

Improving on life is something that humans have always sought to do. The misunderstanding is in the definition of "improvement." We can define it logically or experientially, but not both. If we have slipped into the habit of interpreting our lives logically, we will define improvement as more correct, or that which passes the test of clinical benchmarks, a scorecard, or public acceptance. It is in this state that we become attracted to the pursuits of health, fitness, and diets. There is just so much expert advice to gather and analyze; it is logic's playground.

You can identify logical constructs by their assumption that you don't know enough to act in your own best interest. I reject that assumption. I contend that your natural state as a human is to be imbued with a level of innate wisdom that is more than adequate to the task of maintaining your body and your life as a whole. When you can accept that—even as a possibility—it will reveal much about the nature of logic and its mission to keep you dependent on a universal truth rather than a personal one.

Ultimately, logic is defensive in nature. Logical constructs are satisfied only by endless information gathering that never results in any action because logic perceives all action as dangerous (logically speaking, it is). In this way, logical constructs keep us in fear and work against the change necessary to elevate our experience of life.

Conversely, experiential constructs always begin with the premise that we already know what to do, and upon that knowledge we can always act immediately and in keeping with what contributes to a better experience of life. If we live our lives by the quality of our present experience, a better feeling of it is all we need. Feeling better is the beacon upon which humans were designed to be guided.

Consider for a moment how the Conversation deals with the subjects of health, fitness, and diet. Evidence of a logical construct is hinted at in the tendency to turn them into absolute values rather than relative ones. Absolutes suggest there is a point at which we arrive and become perfect examples of a quality (such as healthy or fit). In the case of health, fitness, and diet, though, those values are never identified.

Even a casual observer of such things can easily see that there is no universally acknowledged point at which we unquestionably arrive at the quality known as healthy, fit, or perfect anything. That fact, all by itself, indicates that there is no justification for using the words "healthy," "fit," or any qualitative absolutes of a diet. But try to get through your day (or even an hour) without hearing or reading one or all of them.

This confusion works well for people with things for sale because it keeps all of the markers for success vague and, inevitably, somewhere other than where you are. When you are dependent on something for sale to tell you how you're doing, the answer is never that you have arrived.

This suggestion that health and fitness are absolutes is a natural extension of logic, which drives the whole notion of health and fitness to begin with. Logic demands a standard for determining correctness, whether the standard actually exists or not. You cannot be "correct" without at least the suggestion that this standard exists. That suggestion comes in the form of the words "healthy" and "fit."

This hinting at absolutes that don't exist is what leads to the assignment of a more-is-better mentality to things for which more is *not* better. A more-is-better approach works only when you, with no dependence on outside influences, know with certainty when you have reached the point where "more" turns destructive.

When the value in question is about the quality of your life, that is something that you, and only you, must determine experientially. When you abdicate the role of experiencer-in-chief and leave it to others, especially those with a profit motive, it will end well for their bank accounts, but not for your life.

The more-is-better mentality in the context of logic leads to obsessions. In the case of weight loss, this belief often shows up as anorexia. Anorexia is the neurological (subconscious) belief that, if a little weight loss brings me some of the recognition I crave, then more weight loss must bring me even more recognition and perhaps even love where there currently is none.

However, if there is no absolute value to indicate we have crossed a line, how much weight loss is enough? When experience is the standard, the quality of that experience provides the answer. Yet, if we fail to check in on that experience, or do not know that it exists—when we cannot honestly answer the question "how are you?"—we cannot identify when we have crossed a line from constructive to destructive. That is the root cause of symptoms like anorexia and other forms of obsessive-compulsive disorders.

Likewise, when there is no easily identified standard for "fit," it is inevitable that we would see the creation of Ultra Marathons and Triple Iron Man competitions as legitimate tests of it. From that understanding, it's much easier to see why some people engage in patently destructive behaviors that also have society's stamp of nobility.

Just in the last few days before I wrote this, an item appeared in the news about a person who had broken the world record for holding a "plank" position for over eight hours. This news was greeted with the usual amount of praise and admiration for the accomplishment, the subtext of which is always the suggestion that this accomplishment is a test of character.

But where exactly is the character in this feat; where is the actual contribution to this person's own life or family, let alone to the world? What truly valuable contribution could this individual have made with the time spent training for this stunt? I cannot identify anything of value in this act other than the obvious satisfaction of the person's ego from all the attention.

In this way, applying the notion of more-is-better to the act of holding a plank position—or any physical performance—reveals what a truly sad waste of resources it is. It is the fitness version of anorexia. In terms of actual contributions to life and the world around us, how long is long enough to hold a plank? The answer is always something less than the world record. We often also glorify the results of anorexia as weight loss right up until the time the anorexic dies. Even then, we know that person suffered greatly for much of the time that society was applauding the effort.

Only when we can acknowledge that the emperor has no clothes and that there is no such thing as "fit" and no such thing as "healthy" will we once again realize that the concept of Aliveness—the ultimate satisfaction of life—is the only legitimate qualifier of these matters. Until then, these remain as phantom notions that are compelling only when seen through the lens of logic, not life.

The Case for Aliveness

I made up the word Aliveness simply because there wasn't one already. We came close to recognizing it when the word "wellness" came on the scene but, again, that word was released into the wild with no test for its meaning. If I perceived the original intent correctly, wellness was a concept that was close to what I'm suggesting. But the lack of any test for it meant that it was immediately hijacked for the purposes of selling every weird alternative practice and product you can imagine, and that fell outside the confines of established health practices.

Aliveness is different because it is both the goal and the test: the answer to the question, "how are you?" For each of us and the lives we live, experience is the only reality we will ever know. Everything else is theoretical. In experiential matters, more is always better only until it isn't. When you stop feeling great and are no longer producing results that benefit both you and the world, you can have ultimate confidence that you have crossed that line. This is not an abstract notion; it's the same understanding as the one that tells you when you are too close to the fire.

Where once the nature of life included all of the elements

for a maximum experience of it, that process has become corrupted by a logical version of it that we have labeled "new and improved."

The actual improvement of this new version, though, is only that it gives us an opportunity to become more specialized, which is a craving of logic. One of the principles of this book is that we can never improve upon the nature of our original design or the daily challenges of life in a natural world. We can only turn our back on them in favor of something less.

This shift in our understanding of life in favor of "new and improved" is the result of the human capacity for the logic of more-is-*always*-better. The sheer magnitude of this capacity is unique in the world of living things. It is responsible for the totality of what we call progress and innovation. In this, humans are wielding a powerful tool that dazzles at every turn, but one that also has the potential to be misused. Each of us, individually, pays a price for that misuse.

What does a misuse of logic look like? This, for example: Humans are the only species that seeks to permanently alter the environment for the sake of convenience and comfort. No other animal does that because no other animal *wants to* do that. It's no coincidence that no other animal possesses the human capacity for logic too. Everything that humans can and want to do, but that a dog would never consider, are all byproducts of logic.

Logic is a concept that is universally perceived as noble. However, the unintended consequences of innovation (the basis for what we know of as progress) are the decimation of the environment and the tragic loss of the natural world we have all observed. These are just two of nature's ways of reminding us that logic can be a tool or a weapon. Therefore, it should be used sparingly and only for its intended purpose: mitigating actual and imminent threats to survival. That is not a message that has arrived for most of us.

In many areas of human life, logic is useful. If you need to solve a math problem, it's easy to see the value of logic as a tool, and it's easy to identify when the problem is solved. But it should never be forgotten that logic is just a tool and not life itself. Those who rely on logic as a source of guidance for their lives will be inevitably drawn to the universal truth of specialization—like holding a plank for eight hours—and drawn away from the personal truth of satisfaction with life.

The questions life asks are never answered with a number or a list, but rather by the personal truth of our experience. That in turn suggests that we should honor everything about nature and the environment and the historical cues from our ancestors as contributors to our overall experience and a great starting point for a maximum quality of life.

Yet, most of us have come to believe that the modern architecture of life is better than anything that came before. Worse, the nature of modern life suggests that sacrificing any of the relative comforts and conveniences we have access to today is an antiquated notion and only for the simple minded.

Consider the possibility that a lifestyle more congruent with historical cues will contribute to nearly every aspect of the human experience. What we must do first, however, is reject the notion that everything modern is superior to everything historic. Then, we merely tolerate, never glorify, innovations of modern life. Our historic lifestyles must remain in our minds as the de facto standard for the way humans were designed to live.

The rest is up to your personal experience, which may sound like an invitation to head home for a night of TV watching from the couch. But just an acknowledgment of Aliveness as a value is enough to drive significant change in the way each person lives personally and the paradigm for society as a whole. It requires a powerful shift to accomplish just that. The result will always be more energy for life, not less.

As the owner of a health club, I spent a large chunk of my life helping people improve the external aspects of their life; physical conditioning is a classic example of that. I coached many of them who were obviously suffering in their internal experience but thought the solution was to dress up the outside. This is logic at work in a human because it was seeking validation outside itself, which is a classic pursuit of logic. Logic's version of satisfaction lies in, among other things, the envy and/or approval of others. Then, treating that approval as valuable information.

Helping someone develop physically, while never addressing the elephant in the room quite literally required me to lie to them. I realized that the inside state was ultimately going to win out in determining the quality of the outside state, and that focusing on the external without addressing the internal was doomed to be a transient and diluted form of satisfaction.

What logic will never tell you is that the only life you will ever know is the internal one. If the process to improve that experience turns out to be an easy one, all the better. But you should know that my intent here is exclusively internal results, identified as elevated levels of fun, love, energy, and creativity that can never be confused with anything else. This is you at your highest potential, regardless of how attractive or correct or easy the process may be, and regardless of how it all looks on the outside.

This explanation isn't a metaphor; it is precisely what's

going on in the world today. We have failed to recognize that so many of the things that bring us recognition and wealth also leave us unfulfilled and unsatisfied with life. I suggest that our pursuits of health, fitness, and a holy-grail diet also fit that description. We are looking only on the outside as a solution to our suffering because we are too frightened to look inside and afraid of what we may find.

Another favorite quote of mine is found in the book *A Return To Love* by Marianne Williamson. She writes, "Our deepest fear is not that we are inadequate. Our deepest fear is that we are powerful beyond measure." I suggest that our focus on health and fitness is an avoidance of our real power, evidence of shrinking from the unlimited power of the human spirit.

Another example of this modern-day focus on the external is that we give people a voice in the world for no other reason than they happen to have acquired large sums of money. They are interviewed on news programs and talk shows, they are paid huge speaking fees, and they are given every benefit of the doubt in a conflict with someone of lesser financial stature, and on and on.

If we have learned anything from history, it is that having a large net worth, however it might have been acquired, does not automatically qualify someone for any other role in society. Yet, in practice, we treat it as if it were an absolute measure of nobility. The wealthy and the recognized may also be fulfilled and satisfied with life but not because of wealth and recognition.

This isn't the fault of the wealthy; they sometimes turn out to be great teachers and an inspiration to others. But money is not the primary evidence or cause of any of that. A far greater percentage of them turn out to act in some monumentally destructive ways.

At the very moment that energy-giant Enron was secretly collapsing under the weight of fraud and mismanagement and taking many Americans' retirement accounts with it, its CEO, Kenneth Lay, was receiving the last of his $220 million windfall in salary and stock, huge speaking fees, and accolades from government officials as a shining example of a successful American.

The reality is that the percentage of the wealthy population that also turns out to be an inspiration to others is no greater than the percentage of the non-wealthy. Yet, the non-wealthy are rarely sought out for their wisdom or guidance. That is the effect of image over substance that reigns in the modern world.

This glorification of the wealthy—specialists in the realm of money making that presumes some level of character and wisdom—is a corruption of our thinking on a societal level. We think money will do the same for us and/or that it is inextricably tied to character, respectability, and the greatest experiences of life. Now I invite you to substitute the word wealthy with "looking fit" and you'll see the relevance of this observation to the world of health practices.

Mostly, what we seek in all our endeavors is a better experience of life. Or perhaps we don't really give a damn about the experience of life as long as we get the recognition. To which I say, "Wow, you must not be good at very many things." Not being good at very many things is another way of saying "not enjoying life to the fullest."

This is why I also exercise great caution with the concept of "leadership." I recognize that there are no leaders in the world except those who are elevated to the role enthusiastically by a multitude of followers. Leadership is a form of specialization. By promoting leadership, we are also promoting the notion of society's designated "winners and losers."

In practice, we look to leaders to do our thinking for us so that we can devote ourselves to our own specialized pursuits—like checkers, for example—that feel safer to us. We also look to leaders because we have lost the ability to trust our own innate wisdom. Whenever you refer to someone as a "great leader," you are also identifying yourself as a "great follower."

Here again we have a concept that, on the surface, appears limited to a few specific areas of life, but actually runs much deeper in the human psyche and affects life broadly. For example, when I talk about leadership most will immediately think about the worlds of politics or business. But when you look at how many people are vying for some form of leadership in the realms of health and fitness, and those of us who will put them there, you see that it is far more pervasive.

I believe the goal of any society ought to be the empowerment of its citizens such that they never need or want a leader, which also means they never need or want to be a follower. That is a subject for a book of its own, but when it comes to your satisfaction with life the only leadership we all need and deserve is the leadership we exercise over our own experience.

All logic is built on the premise that you don't know enough to avoid the threat and therefore need information and/or a leader to be safe. In today's for-profit world, you are never enough. You are constantly being told that you are flawed, misguided, and hopelessly incapable of making good choices and living life to its fullest. But never fear, oh Hapless One, because we have the solution right here, and it's only $149.99 a month for the rest of your life. I know because that was my pitch. But now, I reject that as a message with any power to improve lives.

Can you even recall the last time someone advised you to simply trust your own wisdom on the crucial matters of life? If you're waiting for some external validation that you can trust yourself above all, you'll be waiting a long time. That is because there is no money in this advice. There is money only in convincing you that you don't know enough to live well and therefore you must pay others who (supposedly) do know. This is not something to fear or even be angry about. It just is a fact of our current evolution.

So, this is an overview of the phantom nature of a logical life. Next, we'll take a look at how that shows up in our pursuit of health, fitness, and weight loss specifically. Remember that these are hallowed and revered theories in the societal paradigm, and that challenging the nobility of them—even in your own mind—is as unsettling as challenging the theory of gravity.

But you will also learn that there is a great prize awaiting those who take the journey. A prize that, perhaps, is made known to you for the very first time. As any great adventurer will tell you, the magic is always in the road less traveled.

THREE

Phantom:Health

Key Message:

Every aspect of life that we are seeking to improve by use of the word "health" is already available to us neatly wrapped up in the intention to honor our lives.

It is difficult to find a word that is as universally revered as "health." But before we talk about the word health, we need to distinguish the language from the concept. Language rarely, if ever, represents a concept well, especially a concept as intricate as health must be.

There is no shortage of health advice in the world. The internet is full of it. So is your mother. So is that guy in accounting, not to mention your doctor and personal trainer. If you take it all in, you're left with a big blob of "information," some of it contradictory. What then?

Despite the reverence with which we treat the word, consider how unclear we all are about what exactly health is. There is an abundance of evidence that the concept of health is vague and ill defined, such as the fact that no two people will use the same words to describe it. Other than having something to do with the state of the body, there is not now, nor has there ever been, any exacting standard for the quality known as health.

In the absence of a deep understanding of the concept people feel free to attach the word health to anything and everything they wish to promote. These are usually nothing more than theories that sound like they might be true but are hardly actionable knowledge.

While we always experience health as a personal matter, we treat it and talk about it as if it were a clinical and universal one. We know there is no hard scientific data that unfailingly represents the state we call health, and we know the science that *does* have data already has a name; it's called "medicine."

We allow modern health practices to ignore the personal nature of it because we, ourselves, have become mired in the science, expert opinion, and the numbers that are claimed to suggest health, instead of paying attention to their actual value to our lives. The bathroom scale is a superb example.

This confusion can be likened again to The Emperor's New Clothes. As in that fabled story, the answer is in something that no one wants to be the first to say: in this case, that there is no such thing as health. At least there is no such thing relevant to your quality of life and longevity, which is the only health most of us know.

Many would readily accept that lay persons do not know what doctors and scientists know about correcting disease in all its forms in the human body. But those same scientists and doctors have no claim to any particular knowledge about humanity—especially yours—except that which we give them by using the word health to describe the quality of our lives.

So, what we have is this: doctors proclaiming those with

a tragically diminished degree of Aliveness "healthy" if they pass some clinical test. And, individuals with no scientific background at all proclaiming themselves "health coaches" without adhering to any standard, legal or otherwise.

These two types of health providers each have radically different approaches to the subject, and each will also deny the effectiveness of the other. But both are also very popular; evidence that there is no standard that would help you and I know the value of any advice or proclamation that goes by the name of health.

Even a quick peek under the covers of the data would reveal something very wrong with the concept. But peeking under the covers, and into the layer of experience, is not the job of science. It seems clear the concept called "health" fails the test of science, yet we seek scientific answers to our questions about it. This misapplication of science serves only one purpose: providing justification for portraying the experience of life as something available for debate and mastery.

It's easy to be drawn into the belief that health is something to be mastered. But health is only *a thing* for that reason: to give the human capacity for logic something else to specialize in. This also serves the purpose of providing a new market for products, services, and expert opinion. None of that has anything to do with how you and I experience our lives.

A far more constructive way to view the state of your body is to see it as something that supports the bigger question of your life. Yet, if we are sucked into treating health as a stand-alone scientific question, we will be unavoidably drawn away from that bigger purpose for it. Humanity—how you feel—will always be an inextricable component of your physical state.

How you feel doesn't need a name because naming

something suggests the concept is monolithic in nature. Yet, how you feel is a fluid thing and not static. Whatever name you give it today would have to mean something very different tomorrow.

How you feel, physically and internally, is mostly for your information—it needs no justification and seeks no approval. There is a tremendous amount of information in the experience of how you feel. But, it is not in the form of data, it is in the form of awareness. That is what makes it the best answer to the question, "How are you?"

The reason for all this confusion is that the internal experience of health is always intertwined with a few external markers of health. We can easily identify some external cues, but it is the experience of it that defies every analysis of the data. Neither scientists or lay people know how to assimilate the experience of life into a scientific conclusion about health.

So, it seems we have created the concept of health so that we could talk about the workings of the body without having to commit a decade of our lives to learning that pesky science stuff. It also provided a basis for exercising some degree of control over our bodies, as if they belonged to someone else instead of being our own.

Scientifically speaking, where medicine leaves off and health begins is actually just more medicine. But practically speaking, where medicine leaves off is where Aliveness begins.

Health as a Product

Aliveness is where life becomes a creative process, not a scientific one. If there is recognized dysfunction in the body (and I can't say this enough), see a medical scientist, a.k.a., doctor. If you're not suffering from some diagnosable ailment, it still doesn't mean you are either healthy or unhealthy. You could live to be 150, or you could drop dead from a heart attack tomorrow. Medicine may help to predict the probability of each of those scenarios but being symptom free is not a data point for that prediction.

The rest of life is always and only about our path to some purpose that is ours and ours alone. That is where medicine ceases to have much to offer, but Aliveness knows all.

Although for-profit entities attempt to merge the concepts of medicine and health, there is no health with which to merge other than the idea of it in people's minds. We're mostly attracted to the idea of health because it is one of the specialties I spoke of earlier: a logical form of purpose. The illogical form of purpose is the honoring of life in all ways, not just the physical. Honoring life is a purely creative and unreasonable act.

The modern-day version of health, the one we refer to in the Conversation and the one we practice, is a purely logical construct and is therefore artificial in nature. Or, in language better understood by many, heath is the productized version of what is otherwise a simple component of life. In its original form, the goal of health was no different from the goal of life itself, and the processes for it are innately known and readily available.

The most valuable prize in life is an exceptional quality of it, and the length of it is a distant second. If the choices you make are guided by any other goal it is something less. If you choose to spend your time pursuing cosmetic enhancement (including weight loss), competition, or any of the other bragging rights so common in the practice of fitness and health, that is your choice, and I cannot object to that as a choice. I may refuse to contribute to that cause, but those are choices that each of us are free to make for ourselves. However, I will always object to the suggestion that any of those pursuits are also about the suggestion of health and longevity.

This is significant because it is universally accepted that the pursuit of fitness and sports performance—as they are commonly understood and, most importantly, practiced—also benefit health and longevity. This is a falsehood against which I will certainly rail.

I often made the case with my clients that health and longevity are not benefits of common fitness practices. It was at that point that so many of them backed slowly out of the room, careful not to spook me before they reached the door. We all know what the impact of that would be on the industry known as fitness were it widely known. How many people would stay on the path of modern fitness practices if they became convinced it had a negative or no impact on their health and longevity?

More likely, they would simply refuse to believe it, and anyone can accept that position for the same reason that the industry rejects it. Namely, there is no standard of health that will reveal a positive or negative result of these practices.

The fact that there is no workable and accepted definition should give people enough reason to be skeptical of any claim of health in the marketing of products, services, or practices. But people are eager and willing to believe this claim nonetheless because no one wants to be the first to admit that they don't know what it is. And, when it comes to the claim of longevity, many are seemingly content with near-term cosmetic benefits while the jury is still out.

The real test of health and longevity is the current quality of our experience, but most of us are numb to that quality. We lost that as a reference point in childhood when we were taught that being acceptable to others was the most important goal, and often the only goal that kept us safe in a malevolent world.

Let's break down the meaning of "artificial" and "productized" to better understand the significance of them:

- Artificial is defined as "made or produced rather than occurring naturally, especially as a copy of something natural."
- A product is most identified as "an article or substance that is manufactured or refined for sale."

The term "productized" means to take something that occurs naturally and is an innate aspect of life and reshape it into something that has the appearance of being new and better, whether it is or not. Then, offering this repackaged thing as something more or, at the very least, differently valuable. Again, whether it is or not. This connects the specific goal to the provider so as to be much more difficult to duplicate apart from that or similar providers. But none of this has much to do with you and the experience of your life.

The success of productization depends on convincing people that there is something new here that was not known before and that is unobtainable by any other means. Although this is an effective way to get people to part with their money, how often is it actually true? That is, of course, the claim of all health, fitness, and dietary practices and products. Is it any more true for them?

Again, let's be clear that I am distinguishing health from the science of medicine. And let's always remember that humans thrived in the absence of medicine for countless generations. In those times, the naturally available form of health was all we had and, as the Bible reminds us, it was good.

If you look past the initial marketing language, you quickly realize what most of these products and practices are offering is the ability to compensate for the artificial nature of modern life. But living in an artificial environment and doing artificial things has always been your choice. Do you buy a bandage for your cuts or do you stop cutting yourself with sharp objects?

Products are mostly substitutes for our time and attention and, in some cases, physical effort, but the experience of life is all about time and attention and physical involvement. This is why I say that products for sale are inevitably distractions from life, not enhancements of it. Products free us up to specialize in ways that entertain our capacity for logic rather than enhance the experience of life.

Every facet of life that we are seeking to enhance by use of the word "health" is already available to us neatly wrapped up in the intention to honor our lives. Maintenance of the body and prevention of disease happens not in a hospital or gym, but rather in our individual homes and lives 24/7/365. They are the natural byproducts of Aliveness, the ultimate expression of honoring our own lives in every way that creativity will allow. You carry that quest for a greater degree of Aliveness wherever you go and whenever you go there.

Yet, the word "health" is used constantly in the Conversation and especially in advertising. Despite my commitment to never use the word, I still struggle almost daily to avoid it. I invite you to keep track of how often you hear and use the word on an average day. The number will surprise you. And it's all because the societal paradigm believes that health is a real thing that must be debated and acted upon.

Without exception, the word health is used to dishonor the integrity of life by parsing it from experience; in other words, for things that have no experiential test for validity. That means your money is buying nothing more than a promise. If your true intention is to honor your life in all ways including the physical, a concept like health is not the place to start.

In challenging the use of these words, a great place to start is by pointing out that, although the word "healthy" suggests an absolute value, there is, in fact, no absolute known as "healthy." Are you ready to say at precisely what quantifiable point someone crosses a line from unhealthy to healthy? If so, you would be the first. The fact is that not even the most respected in that field can identify that point in the state of another.

I take this stand on health only because the word—as it is now used—is not just unnecessary, but is a distraction from the prize of a satisfied life. For example, one of the biggest obstacles to Aliveness is thinking we are already healthy. Since there is no exacting measure of that quality, we can and do make that claim to ourselves and others, while hopelessly mired in decidedly destructive practices.

I saw this at work in my own gym. Some of my most dedicated clients—those who had put in a lot of hard work and had the observable changes to show for it—would come into the gym and brag to others about lifestyle choices that compromised their quality of life in other ways, such as drinking binges, risky sexual practices, and addictions.

At the same time, these clients were referring to their own physical condition as "fit" and "healthy" and were referred to by others that way also. So, as long as there were observable cues and no one challenged the label of "healthy," everyone treated these conversations as realistic. Just another example of how the words health and healthy can keep us mired in destructive behaviors.

Creating Aliveness

Creating Aliveness in modern times begins with the awareness that humans were never programmed to think about their health as something separate and distinct from life itself. Prior to modern days the strongest catalysts for proper human function and vitality were found embedded in day-to-day challenges and rewards. These were the unavoidable acts of survival in a natural environment. If people survived, they were de facto healthy without ever using the word or giving a thought to the concept.

Nature's plan was full of hardship and scarcity, but it caused people to thrive in all ways and made the most of their lifespans. Since the mere act of survival was a key contributor to health, survival was the only awareness necessary to keep them in a state of physical wellbeing, no other thought or word required.

Today, layer upon layer of mechanical enhancements and societal edicts have removed the need to engage in those contributory acts and made the goal of survival a guaranteed gift from our intellect. With that change, though, we have also removed the requirements for physical robustness. Although modern life is clearly an attractive thing, that attraction does come at a price.

We have become a slightly spoiled culture in that we are accustomed to simply outsourcing things that don't fit into our busy schedules, such as laundry, gardening, housekeeping, childcare, bookkeeping, car repair, investments, and even gift-giving (when we can get away with it). In our heads, it always sounds like this: "Here's a problem I don't want to deal with. I'll just pay someone to make it go away." Nowhere in this equation is any consideration for what that inconvenient thing might be contributing to the quality of life.

This mindset makes it seem very natural and acceptable to outsource the care of our bodies also. This is what leads most people to take a pill, see a doctor for preventable ailments, or give in to convenience or flavor in their diets. Unfortunately, when it comes to someone's experience of life, outsourcing never works. Only that person, doing the actual work of maintenance and prevention, can produce the highest levels of physical wellbeing and satisfaction with life.

That small matter of unworkability in the paradigm of modern life, however, won't stop the free market from swooping in to meet a demand, even when that demand is based on a false premise. Don't expect these enterprising souls to let on that what they're selling is only a theory about life. The free market is very good at some things; the highest experience of life just isn't one of them.

But there they are, glossy brochures in hand, ready to make the great-sounding claims of satisfying our need for someone else to take the *burden of health* off our hands. We find this outsourcing in a variety of areas, including health clubs and drive-in fast food. We'll buy just about anything that makes the claim we want to believe before we'll actually do the work of life ourselves.

Here's a crucial distinction: As anyone who has ever watched TV or read a magazine knows, the promise is that you can buy health, fitness, and a diet. That promise is stated in both advertising and quotes from experts just about everywhere you look. But no matter how rich you are, you cannot buy Aliveness. Aliveness happens only as a result of a specific set of time-consuming and inconvenient actions undertaken by the individual who will receive the benefits. Anything else is something less.

Aliveness is the one great equalizer in our world, available equally to rich and poor and unavailable equally to anyone not willing to take personal responsibility for it. The great news is that Aliveness also contains all the emotional energy necessary for this involvement without occurring as a chore or imposition but just more of what makes life so great.

Life By The Numbers

In my research, I came across a lecture given by a doctor on the role of science in the search for longevity and quality of life, but I was disappointed that he kept referring to populations as "healthy" or "unhealthy" with no expressed understanding of either of those terms. This was a guy at the top of the scientific food chain, and it was obvious he had not (yet, anyway) mustered the integrity to acknowledge that there was no basis for those labels.

It's just far too easy to continue talking in those terms because no one challenges it, especially when it comes from someone in a lab coat. So use of those words continues to this day and in the highest circles of medicine and science despite the complete lack of any standard by which to identify them.

This usage also raised the bigger question of the definition of "life." We mostly refer to life in the clinical data-driven sense, but we live it in an experiential one. And the two inevitably end at very different moments in time. Yet, it is only the clinical version that gets the attention of science and the Conversation. That's because the experience of your life is yours and yours alone; no one else will ever have anything to say about it. When something is never discussed it is all too easy to forget that it even exists.

In ancestral times, life ended before people wanted it to and while they were still vital. In that scenario, extending the duration of human life would seem to be the holy grail of progress. Then modern life happened, with all its convenience and innovation. An interesting byproduct of these times is that people now routinely outlive their desire for life, a fact of which science—and most of society—has yet to grasp.

It seems obvious to me that a life is better only by the experience of it, not the years of it. I rarely, if ever, hear that point made in any forum on aging, even though it's precisely why "death with dignity" options are now a matter of law in several states. A case can be made for an entirely new value that removes the confusion about experience as the measure of life. That new value is called Aliveness.

To fully understand Aliveness, we all need to ask ourselves: "If there were some scientific breakthrough tomorrow that pushed my life expectancy to 200 years and beyond, would that excite me much?" Many of us don't even want to live as long as is possible now! Therefore, a life expectancy of 200 years would be no news. Yet, this would undoubtedly be the biggest news story of all time. The way most of us speak about aging in modern times would indicate that adding years of clinical life is the only quality of aging that we consider worthwhile. That's a classically logical attitude because it is measured in the universal truth of numbers.

Over the years as a fitness and health coach, I would often find myself in the middle of the weight-loss debate. You know the one: the "best" way to lose weight, the "quickest" way to lose weight, the "permanent" way to lose weight, and on and on. It's an endless and wholly unnecessary debate.

It is unnecessary because a belief in "the way" is clear evidence that people believe being overweight is one of those naturally unavoidable—if undesirable—phenomena, like having wrinkles and gray hair. They also believe that reversing the effects of it requires that we do something *un*natural. But what? This inevitably leads us to adopt unnatural practices that only the "experts" know.

As with all things fitness and health, if you need to lose weight (different from wanting to lose weight for the sake of aesthetics), you already know what to do. In the case of excess body fat, you need only stop doing that which caused the fat in the first place. In other words, being overweight is always the result of something that interferes with the natural process of life and in which you participated. Therefore, simply stop interfering with the natural processes of life.

While that sounds simple, *ceasing to interfere* is not just a new choice because this interference is a symptom of a corrupted internal experience that lives subconsciously. That is precisely the reason we need to put our focus on that which satisfies our experience as the solution to so many physical issues we previously have identified as unwell or unfit.

Instead, we have been taught to believe that, when it comes to our physical world, we are at the mercy of forces out to destroy our quality of life, and that we must fend them off with information and science-based health strategies.

When a client tells me they don't know what they are doing that is causing them to gain weight, my advice to them is, "Stop believing that you don't know." That is not a reality but only a belief that is supported by people who want to sell a weight-loss program or formula.

So the failure is ours in that we have allowed our Conversation to include the concept of health as if it were a thing we should be doing separate and apart from honoring our lives. As you now know, the word health has no meaning, even to doctors. Rather, it is an entirely made-up construct used for the promotion of products and services for sale. Money dominates that conversation.

Yet, contained within the intent of Aliveness is a whole new level of physical wellbeing that is available to each of us at no cost whatsoever. That is the stuff for which there is no word and no need for one. It is always represented by the quality of our experience and the results of our life.

The earlier quote from Deepak Chopra suggests that the use of any word to describe a physical state that doesn't also include our experience of life is actually destructive to the goal. If we can all agree that health should probably be a more valuable goal than just chasing symptoms and/or theories, using the word "health" to refer to all nonmedical concerns of the body is a corruption of the meanings of both medicine and life.

An obvious question is this: "Shouldn't I just practice health in addition to practicing life? What's the downside of that?"

The downside is the corruptive effects of any logical construct. Engaging a logical construct will take you out of the state you need to be in to practice life. Logic is an all-consuming process. Everything in life that feels like a burden or an annoyance is the result of seeing it through the lens of logic. *Burdening* and *annoyance* are two of the ways our humanity communicates with us about the value of something.

We're told practicing health is serious work, the opposite of fun. That's why it requires discipline and will power (or so we're told). These are not fun ideas, and they are not the stuff of life. A quote that powerfully represents the concept of Aliveness is, "Laughter is the best medicine." Laughter is the momentary experience of life fully lived. Laughter is neither reasonable nor justifiable. Such is the character of life itself.

So, our job—each of us, as individuals—is to abandon our pursuit of anything called health and dedicate those efforts to a larger goal that includes a form of physical wellbeing for which there is no word and no need for one. No corporate entity will ever support this idea because there is no profit in it; modern references to health always have a price tag dangling from them.

No matter how earnestly we strive for it, we cannot claim the life we were meant to live by any universal understanding that is based on information, discipline, will power, or sanctioning. Rather, only on our own personal reality: the experience of it all.

FOUR
Phantom:Fitness

Key Message:
If you never heard another word about fitness and never again stepped foot inside of a health club you would still have all you need to live an exceptional life that is free of obesity and other conditions that indicate a failure to thrive.

It's worth a quick reminder about the choice of the word *phantom* in these chapters. Phantom is "an appearance without substance; illusory." The "substance" of life is always and only the experience of it. It becomes a phantom version when it seeks values other than the quality of the experience.

Since we know now that the concept of fitness, as with health, has no commonly agreed-upon definition, people are free to have their own opinions about what it *should* be. That includes people we refer to as "fitness experts". But no one can be an expert on something for which there are no standards or definition. In that reality, people can have only opinions, not expertise.

During my years of fitness coaching, it became clear that every client had his or her own distinct idea of why they were there, which reflected their own understanding of fitness, along with any relevant markers of success. This meant that, rather than the client taking cues from their coach, the coach ends up taking cues from the client.

If coaches don't conform their information and guidance to the intent and goals of the client, there will be a lot of talking past each other. Ultimately, the client will get frustrated and leave. If the coach intends to bring some integrity to the process there will need to be some intensive reeducation to bring the language and intent in line.

The real challenge in all of this is the fact that neither party has any test for their respective understandings other than the specifics of the result. Even talking about goals is problematic, again, because of language; the same words can be used to describe very different qualities. In the end, because this is a customer-is-always-right world, it is far easier and more profitable for the coach to simply adapt their program to the intent of the client.

What does this sad commentary say about the integrity of the qualities known as "health" and "fitness". It says that they are empty words that can mean whatever benefits the speaker. However, we do not acknowledge that reality in any conversation on those subjects. It would be foolish to blame the speaker when the real cause of this confusion is that many of us continue to nod with understanding upon hearing the words "health" and "fitness" when we don't understand at all.

However profound the quality-of-life change I was able to provide my clients, I had to accept the fact that most would have been supremely satisfied to just look better naked. Many actually believed that was the definition of fitness, and the only goal worth the inevitable disruption of their comfortable routine. I found that I cared about those people even more because I knew that the priority to look better naked was only a misunderstanding about the possibility for the work. It is for them that I write this book.

That goal poses a distinct conflict for people in the fitness business who understand and care about the inseparable *whole* person, not just one's physical state. The conflict is that helping someone look better naked is an entirely different process from that of improving quality of life and longevity. Yet, the sheer number of people who want to look better naked dictates most of what personal trainers actually do.

So, it is not the fitness professionals but everyday people who need this distinction. Without it, we can all become convinced that what our egos want is also what our life needs. All the better if it comes wrapped in a catchy name. The distinction isn't just in the process, though; the outcomes are mutually exclusive too. When you work for one, you diminish the other.

The Worship of Fitness

Over the years it took for me to reach the level of owning my own fitness business, I observed that other fitness professionals—including, eventually, my own employees—were entrenched in some serious dogma about whatever particular version of fitness they had chosen to worship.

"Dogma" and "worship" are entirely appropriate words to describe what happens in the fitness world. Nearly everyone devoted to the act of fitness is committed not to fitness but to a particular *sect of* fitness. In fact, we all tend to get a little cultish about our own current version of fitness.

Once we have identified a version of fitness that promises to deliver the qualities we want, that doesn't interfere too much with our comfortable lives, or where our friends like to hang out, we feel compelled to defend that version as the *real* fitness. It is this entrenchment that produces so much debate about the right way and the wrong way to exercise. Remember that it is only our egos that demand this correctness.

Next time you hear the word fitness in conversation, I invite you to ask the speaker directly to support the use of the word by precisely defining it. That is not an unreasonable request, but it will always be met with some degree of annoyance, the inference being that you are nitpicking and looking for a loophole. It's an uncomfortable question only because those who use the word are never challenged to be specific about its meaning.

What I am also saying is that there is no fitness separate and apart from life itself and that which supports the reason that we're all here. There is a non-specific form of fitness that is an intrinsic part of life itself, but because the quality of that life will ultimately determine the quality of that fitness, the word need rarely if ever be spoken of as something separate and distinct. Any other version may be a useful concept in clinical circles where the job is to dissect and analyze elements instead of the whole, but we non-clinicians need concern ourselves only with the question of life itself.

There is no practical reason to distinguish between physical vitality and life vitality, except to say that only the physical version will benefit from this thing known as "exercise". By embracing a focus on the purely physical we lose the beacon that informs our ability to enhance life. That typically shows up as a mindset that ignores vitality as a virtue and proceeds directly to cosmetics and bragging rights.

Where a description of a vital life is represented by being "broadly capable" with no concern for aesthetics, the modern version is represented by cartoonishly artificial aesthetics and wholly unnecessary and useless physical abilities. None of those characteristics indicate anything valuable in terms of how we experience life.

"Broadly capable" is another way of saying "physically non-specialized". It means you possess the basic functionality and physical capacity to perform most if not all functions for which the human body was designed, and that have historically allowed humans to survive and perform useful tasks.

Non-specialized also means that you will likely never be labeled a "champion" or achieve elite status in any specialized activity. The foregoing of bragging rights is the price for being broadly capable, which ultimately translates to being broadly satisfied with life. These are all dictated by an ability to interact with the natural environment, not a piece of gym equipment.

Fitness by any other description or achieved with the help of a machine or purpose-built device not only distracts us from the work of life, but is actually destructive to that life.

In this logic-centric world we have chosen, we are compelled to pursue only those values that bring us recognition and can be measured by universal and (mostly) quantifiable standards. Creating something designed to elicit envy, and to be precisely measured, is the only reason that this work needs to be referred to by a name such as fitness, and the only reason we need experts to teach it.

Authentic interaction with nature isn't what happens in the gym; it occurs (or doesn't) as a result of lifestyle. I saw far too many (most, actually) clients in my gym sabotage whatever benefits they produced from their gym time in the other 23 hours of the day. Any ability to function that also supports your enjoyment of life and the length of that life must be supported by the totality of your lifestyle.

If the quality of your experience is low and you are on a path to an early end, it isn't gym time you need. What is needed is more awareness of why you're here and the joy that life itself affords. This is the mechanism for honoring your life.

Likewise, if you have created some extraordinary physical capacities by virtue of gym time only, they are temporary and fleeting. The qualities it produces will leave you at some point when you inevitably become distracted from your "workouts" and "exercise" by other passions or compelling issues of life. It is the physical state that you can maintain with your lifestyle alone that matters most.

The Survival Standard

To get some perspective on what causes the human body to thrive, put yourself in the world of 10,000 years ago. It really doesn't matter if you don't know much about those times because common sense will tell you what you need to know. Like, that humans were more naturally active and spent far more time outdoors than the people of today. Just the act of securing enough food to eat, finding shelter from the weather, and making modest attempts at improving their standard of living was about all historical humans had the time and energy for. Given that scenario, can you imagine how ridiculous the notion of fitness would be to people of that time?

The general level of activity, the variety of physical challenges presented by the average day, and the necessity of being outdoors for most, if not all, of it produces all the so-called fitness a person ever needs to maintain functional capacity and support the vitality of the body. Any notion of having to set aside time in the day for "exercise"—let alone having a name for it—would be laughable. To people of that time, it was just called Life. It can still be that.

In those days, a robust physical state was both a requirement for survival and an automatic byproduct of day-to-day living. The need to produce a useful outcome through one's individual's efforts was a huge component of that lifestyle. That same criterion will produce the same result for us today. This is the kind of physical conditioning that also produces other profound effects in our lives that logic dismisses as irrelevant. These effects are the many contributions to Aliveness.

As pointed out earlier, in every real way, the domains that make up human life are inextricable from each other, even though the mental/spiritual realms are rarely if ever mentioned in the modern pursuit of productized fitness. In fact, physical preparedness itself is rarely if ever the goal of today's version.

Yet, when understood as a pillar of Aliveness, the condition of the human body can still be optimized in the same way that it always was. Historically, the purpose of activity was not to cause a response from the body; rather, it was always to produce some meaningful outcome, like carrying water, clearing land, moving or toting items over some distance (heavy and light, fast and slow), building shelter, or acquiring food. Those outcomes were not only the reward but also the motivation.

Human activity was dictated by survival first, then by enjoyment of life with whatever time was left over. Those goals required some simple criteria for physical preparedness: The complete range of motion and breadth of movement for which the human body was designed (no picking and choosing favorite sports or "routines"), a broad range of intensities (long and slow to short and fast), and frequent but relatively short exposures to these challenges, interspersed with rest.

Even if you could match all of that in the context of a gym or health club (which you can't), that last one conflicts dramatically with the notion of cramming "exercise" into one-hour periods of two to five days each week. In the real world, physical challenges occurred throughout each day for 5 to 30 minutes at a time, with longer periods of easier (but still functional) movement in between.

You can still create activity that meets those criteria today, but it's easy to see how modern life has corrupted that plan, and how an "appointment" workout frustrates the intent. The modern version of exercise simply cannot and will not duplicate the benefits of legacy activity. Everything about it is wrong: the environment, the tools, the principles, the goals, the motivation, the understanding, and a few other things I can't think of right now.

When I talk about activities that contribute to Aliveness, I'm speaking of principles, not specifics. Talking about specifics misses the point of challenging your body in a way that will enhance the life of the individual, not just to satisfy the edicts of a program. Routines and formulas have nothing to do with you as an individual.

All we really need as a starting point are the principles suggested in historical activity patterns that reflect the realities of life in a natural setting. They probably deserve a book of their own, but here is a brief explanation of the most important ones:

Variety

This is defined as the breadth of activities for which the human body was designed. It is determined first by observing the full range of motion of each of the body's joints, then identifying which activities involve all those movements in the aggregate. Most of these can be identified as useful actions—such as running, jumping, climbing, lifting, throwing, squatting, etc. Another aspect of variety is the environment in which these activities are performed. For example, running may be performed uphill or downhill, for distances long and short, and speeds slow (jogging) and fast (sprinting). Variety also includes whether the primary movements are done separately or in combination.

Randomness

Randomness is defined as the absence of any logical reason for any series of choices. This principle requires that we abstain from anything resembling a program or a pattern for our activity, no matter how scientifically justifiable it may be. It is void of any identifiable reason for engaging in any specific activity on any specific day.

Since patterns are attractive to our capacity for logic, we are naturally inclined to employ them in our choices. Some of the best ways to ensure randomness is to draw our activities out of a hat or by virtue of a roll of the dice. Or, have someone who doesn't know your activity history choose for you. Randomness means you may do the same activity 2 days in a row, but just as likely there will be several weeks between repeating something. In any event, I can assure you your brain will object to this idea, so be prepared for some pushback from logic.

Interaction With Nature

This is the simplest of the principles and can easily be described this way: get outside; as often and for as long as possible. I know it can be cold, wet, hot, or a myriad of other undesirable conditions. But desirability is not the goal here, enhancing your life is. Whatever weather you may encounter is not a deal-breaker except in very rare instances.

Whatever the conditions, please dress for it to the best of your ability, but there are always clothes that will allow you to be outside long enough for some important work to be done.

That interaction with nature is your best insurance that you are engaged in the most constructive physical challenges possible.

Activities Will Mimic Something Useful

Historically speaking our physical challenges were always encountered in the process of doing something necessary to survival for the individual, their loved ones, or their community. At the very least they were necessary to the betterment of life in general. In earlier times, the combination of those goals would fill all our waking hours, and the idea of getting any additional "exercise" would be both nonsensical and unnecessary.

The necessity for activities that serve the interest of survival not only dictates the choices of work, but also the motivation for it. The only real requirement here is that we engage in activities that mimic the requirements of life in a natural environment. That's not really complicated so don't overthink it. In case you believe that this kind of activity isn't relevant in modern life, please remember that the human design has not changed, only the environment in which you dwell. The two no longer conspire together to create a fulfilled life unless you remember your design.

Combined, these principles will prevent you from ever limiting your physical challenges to anything that could be referred to as a routine, a program, a pattern, a sport, or a specialty. And will ensure that you also don't limit the work to artificial environments.

As I'm sure you are aware, many who engage in regular physical activity limit their choices to things they find less onerous for one reason or another. That is a logical approach. Runners tend to *only* run. Cyclists tend to *only* cycle. Rock climbers tend to *only* rock climb, etc. And when there is variety of any kind, it will nearly always turn into a program or a pattern of activities that occur on a schedule and a recurring basis, and that claims to be more effective at producing some result. Only that result never includes a greater satisfaction with your life.

The primary activity and whatever patterns we adopt become part of who we are; a part of our personality. All of this is evidence that we have abandoned our internal wisdom about the most powerful principles for our movement and physical challenges.

In my search for variety in my activities, I added yoga to an ever-expanding list of choices a few years ago. It satisfies the need for function and adds an apparent connection to emotion; part of that "whole person" I speak of.

Just one thing though: I really suck at yoga. I'm so rough at it that I wouldn't ever think of attending an actual yoga class—you know, like with *other people*—simply because I'm certain I would bring the class to a screeching halt while the instructor tried to figure out what the hell was wrong with me. Instead, I converted a room in my house into a yoga studio, and I follow along to "beginner" yoga videos on a wall-mounted tv.

Even after several years of consistent practice I can still only do about half of the poses and transitions that are called for in the typical beginner class. And most of the rest are barely recognizable examples of what is being demonstrated. None of this has changed much from Day 1. Yet, despite it all, I'm proud of this accomplishment.

You may be wondering how I can label a complete lack of progress after years of work an "accomplishment", so let me explain. What I have realized is that just showing up for yoga (or any constructive activity, however, whenever, and wherever that happens) provides a benefit to my life that is alone and apart from whatever mastery of the work I exhibit. The benefit is that it teaches me how to listen to my body. That is a rare quality in modern times, and independent from how masterful I am. I recognize that benefit and claim it as the reason this is an accomplishment.

But the question that begs an answer is: does that benefit increase with the degree of mastery? Surprisingly, not much. In fact, there is the distinct potential for diminishing the quality of life for the sake of that pursuit. Those who are making gains in their yoga prowess might want to take a hard look at their lives and ask themselves what other aspects of a full and exciting existence they are sacrificing for this specialized mission of excellence. There are without question some of those.

I get that it is indeed compelling to want to be great at yoga. Watching those who are exceptional at it will bring out that competitiveness in just about anybody, and make you want to rise to some level of excellence no matter what the cost. That is, at least, until you actually know the cost.

The price for this par excellence is 6 or more yoga sessions a week (yes, the really driven often engage in multiple practice sessions in the same day), plus all the other lifestyle changes that are requisite to the goal. Add to this the inevitable intensive or specialized training courses, private instruction, the bill for all the above, and the sacrifices soon become apparent.

What other aspects of your life must be shelved to make way for this new focus. Is yoga able to replace the joys those other pursuits bring, or even contribute to them? Being great at yoga doesn't guarantee you a better life if your only goal is to impress other people.

If all that gives you pause, I'd like to suggest, as an alternative, that you consider just continuing to suck at it like me. Making the conscious choice to suck at anything—defined as "doing it with no expectation of improvement or recognition"—is actually one of the more enlightened choices you can make.

Just ask yourself how many of those who have been bitten by the competitive yoga-bug would be content to be a yoga schlub like me indefinitely. The unenlightened choice would be to either go all-in for yoga bad-assedness to the detriment of other life-qualities or quit immediately upon learning how bad you are at it.

The real danger is our inability to often recognize when we are pursuing a passion versus when we are slavishly seeking satisfaction of the ego. Are you confident you know into which of those two categories your drive for mastery falls? It's not always easy to identify, but passions can be identified by the answer to one question: Would I still be driven to devote my time, energy, and money to this pursuit if I knew no one would ever observe the outcome of it, or even know about it? If you can honestly answer yes to that question, then by all means yoga-up! It is you the yoga world needs to lead schlubs like me. Just realize that even passions exact a cost for their pursuit.

If you can't answer yes to that question, then you, my friend, are a specialist, and that means you have somehow tied your self-worth to the goal of specialized mastery. That's not fun or constructive, and it won't end as a net gain to your life. I, myself, am relishing my yoga "schlubness", and would consider it a red flag of the highest order were someone to ever tell me I was good at it. That's the moment I would know that I have gone off the rails of my life for the sake of a specialty.

Why Exercise?

To anyone from historic times, it would be readily apparent that we have so corrupted the world in which we live that we can't maintain even a basic level of physical preparedness without some kind of intervention. We call that intervention "exercise," but it isn't really anything but an artificial construct designed to compensate for the damage caused by an artificial world. And frankly, there isn't much of that compensation.

We haven't changed in any significant way since that ancient time. What has changed is our environment. In recent times, we have created a logic-derived artificial world that presents practically none of the physical challenges necessary for a natural level of functional capacity. Functional capacity is the only physical state that also contributes to our overall state of vitality, longevity, and quality of life. This modern world is designed to appeal to only our logical brains, not a thriving life.

Given that our genetic makeup is still very much the same as that of people who lived 10,000 years ago, there is a lot to be learned from remembering this history. That is, any attempt at manufacturing substitute physical challenges for the sake of maintaining optimal levels of function is doomed to be something less. We were designed to function in the natural world. The natural byproduct of that functioning was everything needed to be at our physical best for as long as we are supposed to live.

It is clear then that fitness is a manufactured construct of modern times, not a necessity for a long and fulfilled life. But we still have the option of maintaining our bodies as did the people of historic times. And all those activities are still available to anyone at any time, in any place, and at no cost. Can the same be said for the neon version of the typical health club today?

So, the standards of nature's plan for maintaining our bodies no longer exist in the Conversation. In their place, we have managed to engineer and innovate a world that has no regard for nature or its plan for us. At the same time, we watched our bodies decline into some sad states of misshapen neglect as a result. Then we put ourselves at the mercy of personal trainers and coaches and fitness experts and weird machines in an attempt to recreate what we have lost.

Since we no longer have a true understanding of what a vital human is all about, we have reduced our view to cosmetic values worthy of recognition and only that. The world of fitness as it exists today is a clever way to make money rather than to faithfully restore the system that was designed for us. But the choice is still ours.

The original use of the word "fitness" was to describe somebody who was fit *for something*. Young kids who worked on farms and spent a fair amount of time pitching bales of hay onto the back of a flatbed wagon, for example, developed certain capacities suited to that task. Then it would be said that they were "fit for the job of loading hay."

The point is that, historically, the word "fit" was never used to describe a general condition, and certainly not a cosmetic one. Rather, it described a specific capacity that had been trained in a person. In the past people who were more generally robust were described as "hale" or "hearty". Whatever the task may be (including sports), the process of becoming *fit for* that task is a mind-numbingly simple affair. Those kids with their hay bales didn't even know they were doing it!

Here's all you really need to understand: the human body is a highly adaptive organism. It adapts precisely and predictably to any repeatedly encountered physical tasks in a way that allows it to accomplish those tasks, and only those tasks, more efficiently. Therefore, different types of physical challenges produce different body types and why women and men typically engage in different activities. Presto! You're now a fitness expert!

This process of adaptation is one of the survival mechanisms of the body and an automatic outcome of consistency, complexity, and urgency of movement. In the early days of our species, these physical challenges were very broad and universal. It was only after people began to group themselves into clans that any specialization took place, an even then, it was only a little. Today, of course, we're all specialists, and everything is a specialty.

As a result, we've been convinced that physical adaptation is something mysterious and a matter for "experts" only. But just because some have chosen to make fitness their business doesn't mean you need what they're selling. Some things just aren't sophisticated enough to require much expertise. The optimal functioning of your body for life is one of them. Optimal is what serves your purpose, not having a cover-girl/boy appearance, being the victor in a competition, or achieving a cookie-cutter, more-is-better numerical score on some arbitrary physical test.

The Cosmetic Standard

Shredded, ripped, jacked, pumped; this is the language of modern fitness, and the essence of cosmetic results. These words have become the de facto standards for the intent of our exercise. What human qualities are these describing other than how someone spent their time?

Given similar starting points, anyone willing and able to spend all day, every day in a gym (shockingly, many do just that) can be guaranteed of achieving the better-than-average physical cues we know of as fitness. So, how special are those qualities? And why do we glorify them? They are, in fact, among the most mundane and predictable of all accomplishments. Yet, the ego is very happy indeed.

The cravings of the ego are easily mistaken for purpose and meaning in life, but I can't find any significant difference between someone being a gym rat for the sake of appearances and someone being a workaholic for the sake of a promotion. Both are essentially strategies to avoid dealing with the bigger issues of life. And both could easily spot the misguided priorities of the other but yet cannot find it in themselves.

Make no mistake, during my time as a gym owner, I rather liked being muscular and relatively athletic, but I mostly liked those parts of it that others were likely to notice, comment on, and envy. I finally realized that there wasn't much about it that I really cared about except the compliments.

Any exceptional level of conditioning just wasn't useful to my life in any other way, which was an obvious sign that the part of me that liked that was just my ego. The buzz you get from those compliments is the same feeling you have at age 35 when you get carded buying alcohol. Beyond the flattery of being mistaken for someone under 21, everything else about getting carded is just a nuisance.

I could have justified my own conditioning by claiming that I was setting a good example for my clients, and it's a common expectation for trainers to be examples as well as educators. But what does that say about the clients' personal motivation for the work and the goal? The real value of an "example" is in the appearance of it, and it is just more evidence that the construct of fitness is an artificial one that really has nothing to do with the life of the individual.

Now, two important points about what I've just said:

First, not everyone who visits a gym or health club falls into the category I've just described. The issue is not right-or-wrong, gym-or-no-gym but rather recognizing who we are and what life is about. Those of us who do have a grasp on the answers to those questions will likely spend less time in the gym and more time living our lives. Which means that the observable results will be modest at best, and certainly not the "fit model" look of men and women we see gracing the covers of magazines. But, modest or exaggerated, they are still only appearances and not substance.

Second, I'm not suggesting that you allow your body to unnaturally disintegrate into the marshmallow-like form that has become so common in modern life. That is no more or less artificial than the exaggerated "look of fitness" that earns society's mark of nobility and, in the same way, corrupts our notion of what serves our life.

We can achieve the appearance and conditioning that serve the goals of purpose (vitality and functionality) and longevity without ever stepping foot inside a gym or health club. A body that is vital and functional is merely a body with integrity and one that has been challenged in the pursuit of useful activities. The physical contribution to purpose is a body with appropriate levels of integrity, which is precisely the point of all activity that supports our humanity rather than our Instagram likes.

Artificial appearance standards have produced a great public outcry because of the very real psychological damage that occurs to young females who believe idealized images of women presented in advertising and fashion are a de facto standard for acceptance. Despite the claimed outrage, it must be apparent by now that what happens in most gyms is an admission that we have bought into those artificial standards for both men and women and continue to devote massive amounts of time and money in pursuit of them.

I do not suggest doing the bare minimum to avoid looking "out of shape," but we need to revise our understanding of why we need to be active at all. When we make that shift, we realize that being active in the way humans were designed to be active is not a means to an end but an elevation of life through new and different experiences, and the accomplishment of something useful.

The only reason you would need to consult with an expert about improving on your activity is precisely because you have chosen to pursue something other than that which serves your purpose in life. This is why one of the first questions most personal trainers will ask of new clients is, "What are your fitness goals?" This is a thinly camouflaged way of asking, "What type of conformity that clearly has nothing to do with you do you want to achieve?" The notion that fitness is a cosmetic or performance pursuit persists only because no one questions this premise.

As I write this, I see a growing trend of people marketing themselves as "physique coaches." Because the name pretty much says it all, I don't need to explain that except to say that I admire their honesty. Use of the word "physique" essentially means that they have dropped any pretense that the results are about a quality other than appearance.

This approach isn't new; it has appeared before as bodybuilding, with the slightly less cartoonish "natural" bodybuilding variant, in an attempt to satisfy those for whom cosmetics have become the only thing worth working for. Even so, humans apparently weren't satisfied with just one corruption of the concept; amazingly, we have even managed to turn our physical appearance into a competition!

Although this trend should be a disturbing blight on the notion of fitness, instead, it simply adds itself to the ranks of so many other practices that have been absorbed under the banner of fitness so that gyms and health clubs can profit from them. The plain truth is that physique coaches are what personal trainers have always been. We didn't talk about the end result much because the goal of cosmetics was just assumed.

This trend should come as a surprise to no one, especially since the words "sculpt" and "sculpting," as in "body sculpting," crept into the fitness lexicon some time ago and were quickly embraced as a legitimate fitness practice. Just like bodybuilding, the whole notion of sculpting is purely cosmetic, yet seemingly no one was willing to say the emperor was naked.

The truth of the matter is you do not want to look like a fitness model on the cover of a magazine; you can move in that direction, but you don't want to. To explain, let's start with the fact that the most intriguing thing about that look is that it is on the cover of a magazine (or, otherwise widely displayed). That's significant because it implies a standard for acceptance. After all, no one is asking *you* to pose for the cover of those magazines. As a practical matter this is designed to make you feel bad about yourself and the way you look so you'll spend money in an attempt to achieve the same look for yourself.

But the fact is that you do not want to undergo the lifestyle change that look requires. First, it is probably genetically impossible, just like it's probably impossible for you to be a world class ballerina or gymnast due to genetics alone and having nothing to do with your character or work ethic. But, more importantly, the lifestyle that it would require for you to even try has nothing to do with your reason for being alive.

I'm all about lifestyle changes when the goal of those

changes is to support an actual purpose in life that is going to be a lasting legacy for you, and a contribution to the world in general. But a lifestyle change required to look like a fitness model is never about that. Even if you have the proper genetics that lifestyle change is bound to be a drastic and consuming one. We all must ask ourselves what is being neglected in the pursuit of something fleeting and purely cosmetic.

If those images have you believing that the models walk around looking like that under their clothes every day, I have news for you. I have known fitness models in the past who have confessed that on the day of their photo shoots they are not happy people. They hype their bodies for that look with a precise periodization plan of lifestyle changes leading up to those photos; none of it particularly appealing.

In the 10 to 14 days leading up to a photo shoot those models are on an extremely strict high protein and low flavor diet mostly consisting of meat and lightly steamed vegetables with no seasoning or other enhancements, if they eat at all. They typically also subject themselves to several aerobic workout sessions a day during that time and must abstain from—or add to—their lives in many other ways that are not typical, even for them. In the 48 hours prior to the shoot they cut off their water intake to become purposefully dehydrated which gives their muscles more definition. These are behaviors most 10-year-olds would likely advise against.

The point is the rippled muscles and zero bodyfat look fitness models present on photo day is not the look they walk around with all the time, and that would be even more destructive if they did. By the time the photo shoot comes around they are cranky and suffer from all manner of the bodily withdrawal symptoms of being malnourished and malcontent.

So much so that most of them admit to binging in some decidedly inadvisable ways beginning immediately after the final picture is taken.

Not only is looking like a fitness model—or even anything close to it—just a cheap cosmetic trick, even that isn't sustainable. Nothing about it approximates behaviors that contribute to a quality life, either before or after the moment the shutter clicks.

This is just the story of the fitness models, which most people distinguish from fashion models. But that distinction is only a matter of type, not degree. We are all aware of the destructive habits of fashion models for whom being tragically thin and fragile is a requirement for success; how fashion models smoke cigarettes and drink diet sodas as a distraction from food. Regardless, we also know that the fashion model look is still the target for many women despite the obvious toll it takes on their quality of life.

This is the story of exchanging the quality of life for a paycheck and/or recognition, and it is nearly ubiquitous in modern times. It occurs in every walk of life from careers to relationships. But there's a common cause here that is so important: We have forgotten what a quality life is and why we should seek that and only that.

The answer is also the purpose of this book: to remind you that your life is too valuable to waste it chasing recognition or even money. That is a fact that is too rarely brought up in the Conversation, and it is the only awareness that can compete with the bright shiny objects of acceptance and wealth, or even the promise of them.

If all people measured the value of their lives by the standard of fitness models on the magazine covers, no great books would have ever been written, no beautiful paintings would have been finished, and no stirring music would have ever been recorded. Instead of practicing and perfecting their contributions through imagination, and then digging deep into their souls for inspiration to create the next new masterpiece, the artists would all be at the gym doing crunches and bench presses, taking aerobics and butt-sculpting classes.

Artistic creations are contributions to the world that make it a better place for all of us. Meeting the goals of looking like a fitness model seeks recognition for only itself.

The Performance Standard

Let's not ignore the performance version of this obsession. There's no better example I can think of than the act of running a marathon. Running marathons is an eminently doable proposition for just about anyone, but the societal paradigm has elevated it to the level of a respected accomplishment for highly motivated and elite athletes.

Because athletic conditioning was my specialty as a coach, I was often approached by clients with requests to train them for a marathon. It was apparent to me that most of these clients chose this pursuit because they perceived it as something virtuous and therefore indicative of success in life. Many even spoke of it as if they intended it to be the crowning accomplishment of their lives, as in a bucket-list item.

If an internal experience of success has so far eluded people, it's easy to see how they could turn to something external as a path to, or a substitute for, it. To complicate things further, the recognition we heap on marathon runners sounds even more appealing to someone who is suffering a crisis of diminished self. But the achievement of running a marathon is only a theory about success.

Beyond mustering some heightened discipline to see you through the training, running a marathon says very little about your body or your life. In other words, it is such a common accomplishment that there is little about it that is unique to you as an individual. Compare that to the experiences that cause a life to be fulfilled. Fulfillment is a pursuit that is exclusive to you and, therefore, rare to the extreme.

As someone who has a better-than-average understanding of physiology, I could easily argue against running a marathon based on the potential for injury alone; not so much from the actual event, but from the training most undertake to raise their performance in that event. That training is most often rushed and non-individualized. Both are destructive to the integrity of the body.

There is, of course, the repetitive movement of running and the environment in which the training and the marathon itself must take place; namely, hard, flat surfaces. The human body was designed for neither. Although one or two marathons probably won't do any lasting damage, five or ten more likely will.

The bigger problem is that these cautions rarely matter to those who are secretly using this work as an antidote for some deep internal void in their lives. It is unlikely that warnings about physical damage will deter someone who believes that activity will resolve suffering of another kind.

A metaphor for understanding conditioning is looking at the body like a lump of clay. Within certain limitations, you can mold or shape it any way you choose. The more specific you are about the result, the more time and effort and (probably) money you'll spend to get there. Once you really understand how simple it is to shape and otherwise change your body, the pursuit suddenly loses its mystery and appeal.

And it is mostly the supposed mystery of it all that attracts us to the process. It is wanting to "win the game" of health, fitness, and diet that we seek. Yet, it is actually a stone-simple process of adaptation to a consistent and specific environment. But then what?

Eventually, you and your body will go home and once again be alone in the world of your experience. How much do the cosmetics or even performance matter when you are alone at night? It's right about then that you will likely realize how much of your real life—the life that is lived within yourself—has been neglected for these ego-driven goals of recognition.

Notice I said, "within certain limitations." What are those limitations? I'm a bit ashamed to admit that it took me nearly 10 years into my physical development training and practice to realize the role of genetics on absolute performance. By that time, I was coaching others full time and seeing that many of my clients could easily outperform me in certain capacities after just a few months of conditioning and skill work.

It was a bit demoralizing to realize that all of my academic education, hands-on learning, and personal effort didn't automatically guarantee me a spot as a top performer. How could this be? Aren't we told that all athletes become champions by hard work and dedication, and that those who work the hardest are always the ones who excel at anything physical?

I possessed a good understanding of physiology and human performance, I got to dwell in the practice of it daily, and I worked on my own development far more than the clients who could routinely outperform me. In my own life, I saw this so-called universal truism of hard-work-equals-being-the-best as one of those things that sounded like it should be true but in real life simply is not.

Mind you, I didn't feel cheated, and I didn't regret the work I had done and continued to do; there were rewards for the time and effort, but they weren't in the form of being a top performer or a "champion" in any category. I just had to acknowledge that the lesson is false and adjust to the new reality that there were other factors at play here that were rarely spoken of because it was "bad for business."

You see, the business of health, fitness, and nutrition requires that trainers keep the dream alive in the minds of their clients. That dream of being better than others in terms of performance and/or cosmetics is the primary thing that makes a fitness coach worth the money. Then, if the dream fails to materialize, clients view themselves or their coach as a failure when, in fact, there was no drive or intention to sacrifice so much of life for an artificial goal.

Besides intent, the only real failure was one of age, lifestyle outside of the gym, genetics, or all three. The most obvious examples of this are how physically similar all gymnasts are to each other, not just their development but their genetic proportions and propensity to develop certain parts of their anatomy. Another version of this is the zero crossover in specialized capacities between ballet dancers and competitive shot-putters. Zero. Why is that?

You guessed it: genetics. Each sport has its distinct and mutually exclusive requirements for body type. This began when the discipline was itself dictated by a particular genetic type, such as short and muscular for a gymnast or long and willowy for a ballet dancer. Then, and only then, did the work itself apply the finishing touch. No athlete can entirely circumvent their genetics to reach elite or even highly competitive status in their choice of sport.

For there to be subsets of fitness that are dependent on individual pursuits such as a specific sport, other aspects of this fitness will certainly be sacrificed in the process. You can't be both a champion distance runner and a weightlifter in the same body; they are mutually exclusive goals. Yet, they are both routinely referred to as "fitness," as are activities as varied as Iron Man training and kickboxing. So, the question should be, what else are we excluding by pursuing any of those specialties?

While the notion of fitness forces us to choose, Aliveness provides an opportunity to address all the potential contributors to life with the application of just few simple principles. When you embrace those principles in your lifestyle, you also will never be overweight, you will never be incapable, you will never be lazy, and you will never be anything but thrilled with life. To become mired in the minutiae of the process or even the concept is to be concerned with being better than others in some easily recognizable way.

If the modern model of fitness offered a real and valuable quality, instead of "fitness goals," there would only be the quality known as fitness. The phrase "fitness goals" is an admission that there is no universal quality known as fitness.

Likewise, if you are moving your body for the goal of a better experience, there is no need for a new set of disciplines to achieve it. Whatever type and degree of activity is needed for Aliveness would be an automatic byproduct of the quest. This difference changes everything about the activity you engage in to achieve it.

Better still, if the truth is that there is no fitness, why are we talking about it, debating over the processes for achieving it, programming it, selling it, buying it, advertising it, building places to practice and train it, and ultimately sacrificing massive amounts of our precious time and resources pursuing it? It's a phantom notion in the truest sense of the word.

When coaches train athletes for competition, success also is determined by what is happening between clients' ears. Beyond the first month or so of acclimating clients to the scope of work that needs doing and the small number of technical matters specific to the sport, the coach is a minor part of the process. Navigating that strange and wonderful world of beliefs, egos, fears, expectations, and general misunderstandings, far more than the actual training, becomes the job of the coach.

By 2005, athletic conditioning had overtaken aerobics as the most popular form of fitness training and was promoted with slogans such as "train like an athlete." Even though marketing like that brought a lot of new clients into my gym, training like a professional athlete is pointless unless a person is, or seriously intends to be, a professional competitive athlete. As a result, a large number of people would show up wanting to train like the pros but seriously lacking in that same level of commitment and/or bodily integrity. That's a recipe for disaster at worst, or just plain futility at best.

The notion that training like an athlete is a solution for bigger issues of life is no accident. This idea of conducting our lives like professional athletes is constantly being promoted in self-help and personal development circles as a key to wealth and business achievement. In your own reading, you may have noticed that competitive sports are universally used as metaphors for success in life by nearly every success- or life-coach and motivational type.

As a purely practical matter, training the average person like a competitive athlete is to invite injury and obsession, and I can't decide which is worse. The truth is that athletes have an entirely different mindset from that of the average nonprofessional, and it's not a good one. An athlete's mindset is based on the concept of competition, a belief that it is noble to dominate others.

Clearly, training like an athlete carries a lot of baggage with it. The attraction to the training is often based on the idea that the discipline involved has a life-enhancing benefit; that is, it will provide a competitive edge in all areas of life. I can assure that just the opposite is true.

Let's define "athlete" as someone who is involved in a structured game with clearly defined rules and goals, and spectators pay to observe the process. This game is performed for money (or the promise of it), and winning is the only acceptable outcome for both athlete and spectator.

The goal of a competitive athlete is to physically dominate an opponent. If that is not your goal, you will be a mediocre athlete at best. But being a mediocre athlete is a good thing if you want to do more for the quality of your life than the average professional athlete. It also means that you will have no need for the words "fitness," "health," "diet," "competition," or even "sports" in your quest for that better experience. These are constructs that are irrelevant to an authentic life.

Humans in general seek to dominate others only in response to a perceived threat to their own lives or self (the basis of ego) and as a means of escaping that threat. The goal of dominating just does not exist in the paradigm of a mutually constructive and supportive environment. Other cultures—all Biblical notions aside, the Amish, for example—promote an environment where people are responsible for every other person's success as well as their own. This is a spirit of cooperation and support, not competition and dominance.

Yet, our dog-eat-dog culture in modern times, especially in the United States, promotes this notion that other people are enemies to be vanquished instead of friends to be cherished. This sets up the paradigm of needing to silence and incapacitate others for the sake of our own perceived safety. This is the paradigm of sports and the culture of competition that we have fostered. What serves the quality of our lives is to never forget that perceiving that life is under constant threat is never a comfortable, peaceful, or happy place to be. More on this in an upcoming chapter.

Just being active doesn't make you an athlete, although the world of marketing language loves to refer to those of us who challenge ourselves physically as "athletes" regardless of whether the name fits the above description. It's true that challenging activity is a regular part of a fulfilled life, but actual athletes live by rules that do not support life; all their rules support the theme of "winning is everything."

Although that theme sounds laudable and is always presented with nobility as the subtext, it is in fact an attitude that requires major compromises to your overall quality of life. Your activity will be about competition *or* your life; it cannot be both. I won't question your choice, but you should. I'm here only to let you know that a choice must be made.

Before you choose, here's a good thing to remember: Unless you are making money at your activity, you are never going to be a "winner" in the athletic sense of the word. Since the mantra of competition is "winning is everything," it seems wise to question sacrificing your time and money for something that has no value other than the bragging rights of being better than someone else.

No doubt there is a certain satisfaction in winning, but that is a satisfaction of logic (read: ego) only, which often masquerades as satisfaction with life, and even happiness, to those who have never experienced the authentic version. And no matter how many competitors there are in any given challenge, there is only one winner. Who came in second? No one remembers.

When the recognition for being a "winner" in the eyes of others is the goal, what remains for all the discipline and hard work for those who came in second or later? Based on the look on their faces, it is mostly despair and depression.

We all know of the compromises athletes make for the sake of winning: taking performance-enhancing drugs, suffering brain damage, enduring unnatural training practices, and facing the consequences of the repetitive nature of the sport itself. None of these compromises are even remotely about the goal of health or quality living. How they ever became attached to fitness and health—not to mention a quality of life—is unclear, but I hope by now, no one equates athletics or athleticism with character, success, or a quality experience of life and longevity.

This equation is tempting and easy to believe, but it has value only to those who devote their time and energy to a theory about life instead of doing what satisfies them personally. Being a champion is code for being a winner, which in turn is code for dominating other humans, which results only from willingly engaging in competition. This is evidence that the concept of dominance over other humans has become the metaphor for modern life.

When star athletes are interviewed, they are often asked about the secret to their success. Usually, they point to things like a commitment, dedication to training, or will power. They say these things because athletes don't want to disappoint people who believe they had an intentional formula. And those same people very much want to believe that success is a formula that can be copied.

Then, those who promote athletics as a metaphor for life will seize on these answers as evidence that the way to succeed in life is through hard work, grit (whatever that is), discipline, and an unwavering dedication to being "the best." Personal-development coaches love this idea because it just sounds like something that should be true, no one can ever disprove it, and it can be productized as wisdom.

You can be forgiven if you are invested in this theory about success, but the truth of the matter is there are so many variables in the makeup of an elite athlete, or any brand of success, that no one has ever identified the precise formula for greatness. However, everyone interested in defining it wants to believe that the successful athlete has some secret to life that can be passed on to others and that, of course, can be copied.

Even if athletic greatness were simply a matter of extraordinary commitment, wouldn't you have to feel at least a bit of sadness for someone who would be so committed to a purely physical goal that is the equivalent of window dressing? Rarely have I heard anyone speak of a physical accomplishment for its own sake. When I say, "for its own sake," I mean an accomplishment that was pursued for the journey that is directly linked to a better experience of life.

Rather than carve out a part of your day to work for a physical goal, you can pursue a dedication to Aliveness in every moment of every day. Anything that contributes to your Aliveness will find a place in your life, and it won't be because you possess some manufactured discipline or willpower; rather, it will be because you serve a higher cause for which there is greater emotional connection.

Then ask yourself if the theory about commitment sounds plausible. Is it true that literally nothing ever got in the way of an athlete's commitment to a performance goal? No sick child ever needed caring for? No outside passions ever demanded some nights and weekends? No friends wanted to catch up and no creative pursuits needed to be nurtured? Any accomplishment that requires someone to sacrifice those very real parts of life suddenly doesn't sound so noble.

The more honest answer is this: By the time someone reaches the ranks of professional in the world of sports, there has likely been a natural culling process. At the root of this process is genetics. No matter your intent or determination or commitment or grit or any other quality touted as "keys to success" in athletics, you will simply never perform at the highest level of a sport without some genetic advantages. A world-class gymnast is never 6 feet 4 inches tall. A champion hurdler is never 5 feet 4 inches tall.

In the same way, a pro-level lineman in football will not succeed as a ballet dancer no matter how hard he works for it, and a top-flight wrestler will likely never be a competitive distance runner. Those are just the realities of genetics and sport-specific training. Elite-level athletes are most often steered toward their chosen sport by genetics first. Only later are the best of the best determined by training and some level of discipline and determination.

In that sense, if society touted being an accomplished ballerina as a measure of success in life, the football lineman would be considered a failure at worst or simply unaccomplished in the broader realm of success. Putting fitness in its proper perspective means that, just as the lineman is not a failure or unaccomplished, you are not a failure or unaccomplished if you seek only the personal experience of it.

I heard a report on the radio recently about an event known as the "NFL Combine" where scouts evaluate new players for their athletic ability in the context of football. One of the tests is a barbell bench press using a standard load of 225 pounds. The test is to complete as many full chest-press repetitions as possible. Scores in the low to mid 20s are typical for an NFL lineman, with a small percentage of scores at 30 and above. The story I heard was about someone who exceeded that by some extraordinary amount (I believe the figure was 45, but don't quote me).

It's easy to be very impressed by that accomplishment and to believe that it represents something important for human life. After all, it is a sanctioned test for an NFL player. In reality, the only thing significant about it is that relatively few people bother to train for it, so being one of them automatically puts a person in an elite category.

But as a former strength and conditioning coach, I often had to remind people that, unless you're planning a career in professional football, this feat holds very little value for your life. In fact, pursuing it actually has the potential for diminishing your quality of life by virtue of potential injury, and the training will take you away from other important pursuits of life.

If you're a hopeful NFL lineman, no question you'll need to be good at a bench press. (Ironically, that specific capacity doesn't even hold much value for the sport, but it somehow got adopted as a standard test for players nevertheless.) Is playing professional football not in your five-year plan? Marvel at what the human body is capable of when properly trained but give no other thought to the feat.

Yet, even those with no NFL aspirations are often compelled to pursue some degree of excellence in this test. Because it is no longer about football, there must be another motivation for putting that much effort into a goal that will not result in a multimillion-dollar pro-athlete contract. That motivation can be one of only two things: either a misguided notion of what it will contribute to the person's life or the egoic lure of the bragging rights associated with the accomplishment. I would suggest that neither is a valuable use of your precious life.

The Aliveness Standard

If you're willing to reframe the word "fitness" to exclude cosmetics and bragging rights (which includes performance), the purpose of it would be quality of life and longevity. In short, Aliveness. For non-athletes to pursue athletic goals is to delude themselves into thinking they are athletes or to believe that they are addressing their purpose in life at the same time. Aliveness will never put many people in the stands or clients in the gym.

Feeling great as a long-term outcome is the only guidance you need in choosing your activity. Truly constructive activity is not classically measurable and therefore cannot be compared with the activity of other people. For the goals of maximum quality of life and longevity, you already know what to do, and you already have everything you need; no tape measure, no bathroom scale, no maximum loads, no "stuff for sale," and no coaches are necessary.

So, is there any constructive purpose to all these fitness businesses? I'll let you decide.

For starters, you already know you need to move more

often and in a more natural environment than you currently do. You also know how much modern life—not to mention our modern aversion to discomfort and inconvenience—discourages that plan. And if you've been convinced that quality of life is incomprehensible to the average person, you'll likely just give up and take to the couch. That approach, or some version of it, is where most of us are.

Then there's this: The holy mantra of business is "giving the customers what they want." That's an obvious and simple strategy for success in any business, but it is also the reason there must never be a place for profit in the matter of Aliveness.

The scenario that is never addressed is this: What if customers want something that is based on a falsehood or misunderstanding and yet widely promoted for the purpose of justifying a profit center? In other words, how do you reconcile the needs of business with the concepts of ethics and integrity? The fact is, you don't, but they will need to be reconciled at some point in every business. To ignore the conflict is to contribute to the falsehood.

Entire industries are built on false notions of health, fitness, and food programs that sound like they should be true but exist only as a strategy for profit. You may have noticed that most of these fitness businesses are not much more than social clubs wherein alcohol is replaced with some kind of discipline, information, and activity. And the reason they exist is not any more sophisticated or important than your neighborhood bar.

In order to sell the manufactured constructs of fitness and health, marketers have concocted a story about the nobility of it all. This story starts with the idea that you are helpless to preserve optimal levels of your life. Once you've been convinced that you don't know enough and that, even if you did, you don't possess the proper motivation or discipline to execute the process, they trot out all the earnest fitness entrepreneurs who can sell it to you.

The sell job is centered on the notion that fitness, health, and diet are noble pursuits that only those of exceptional character will ever excel at. Whether the stated goal is cosmetics or performance, to "excel," of course, is always and only based upon the degree of recognition it produces.

The establishment of value for the business of fitness has to do with convincing you that it won't happen without the so-called experts and their so-called health clubs. One of the tactics for this is convincing you that fitness is a discipline instead of an honoring of life. Discipline implies massive amounts of time doing something you don't want to do: workouts in the gym, on the playing field, or in other aspects of your life, depending on the specific goal. That's in addition to whatever money is involved for equipment, coaching, and clothing.

Some of that time, money and dedication goes on even in the context of Aliveness, but the degree and intent of it makes a huge difference in how they are experienced, the results of the activity, and your attitude about the work. The Aliveness intent would never describe the activity as a "discipline", and it would never care how much recognition it attracted.

Greatness is never the result of seeking recognition. If you want to cosmetically enhance your body, be a great and contributing person first. Great and contributing people are writing books about some passionate aspect of life, creating great works of art, including music and poetry, and finding ways to alleviate suffering wherever they find it. When you're a contributing person first, you will probably no longer care much about those six-pack abs.

Just using a little honesty in your own thinking, rather than allowing yourself to be caught up in the mass glorification of things that are merely temporal and miss the point of life, can work wonders in improving the point of *your* life. Life is never a rigid path in pursuit of a goal (the definition of commitment). Rather, life is fluid and transient, changing from moment to moment as you respond to the world around you and those you love who are a part of that world.

It is fine to work for a goal; it is finer to work for a life. In that plan, when you are called away from a goal for the sake of a life (some experiential need of yours or someone else's), you can always go back to the goal when the need is satisfied. The only contradiction here is the artificially glorified concepts of commitment and discipline. These are logical values, not human ones.

So, discipline is what you bring to a pursuit designed to appeal to someone other than you, and it opens the door for the destructive, but seemingly unavoidable, consequence of perceiving fitness as a matter of "commitment." It promotes an approach of fitness-as-obsession as opposed to fitness-as-life. Nearly all of us have known one of these obsessed types. Now you know how to not be one of them.

The Language of Aliveness

As I mentioned earlier, I decline to use the word "exercise" or "workout" to describe physical activity that contributes to Aliveness. Like "discipline", these are constructs that only appeal to those seeking that better experience of life but can't quite put their finger on the source of it. Instead, I prefer to reference it as "activity" or "physical challenges". Those words describe concepts that have existed as long as humans have been on the planet and will also contribute to a life of no regrets.

The goal of our activity is the same as it always was: To support and maintain our physical readiness for survival and reproduction in the natural world first, and then to pursue whatever purpose brings us joy and contributes to the world. This description is inseparable and indistinct from the notion of honoring our lives. That is how humans are designed, and that design has not changed regardless of the artificiality of modern life. So, if our design has not changed, why should the nature of our activity or other choices that are routinely made for the sake of fitness?

For the goal of health, fitness, longevity, and an overall state of thriving, there never need be any kind of physical challenge that would not have been both possible and required in the earliest era of humans' presence on the planet. Essentially, that is moving our bodies, and occasional loads, through a natural environment (read: outdoors and on natural surfaces) in as many different degrees and combinations as possible.

In those earliest times, this was also a description of the pursuit of some goal designed to ensure survival and contributions made for the modest betterment of people's own lives or the lives of others. It is safe to say that modern-day "exercise" is never described that way.

If you never heard another word about fitness and never again stepped foot inside of a health club, you would still have all you need to live an exceptional life that is free of obesity, premature degeneration, and other conditions that indicate a failure to thrive.

Frankly, you didn't even need to hear me say that; you already knew it because it's part of your DNA. The only reason we act as if we don't know is that we have been distracted by the message that we don't know, and that we need the modern world's "team of experts" to show us how.

In my experience, the primary benefit of any challenging activity is that it invites us to become more aware of, and therefore more attentive to, our bodies. Physical challenges have a wonderful way of waking up our innate wisdom and focusing it on the state of our bodies. This awakening then gently and thoughtlessly compels behaviors that support and protect a vital physical state.

All physical challenges produce this benefit, but those that are inherently noncompetitive and therefore nonjudgmental seem to be better at it. Any form of exercise that is competitive by nature or design will do far less of this natural refocusing of awareness because the intent of it is no longer about us and our enjoyment of life, it becomes something that is about satisfaction of the ego.

As soon as the logical construct of competition enters the intent of human activity, the act becomes one of sacrificing our bodies by becoming numb to them for the sake of winning. The noble-sounding notion of "playing hurt" or "playing through the pain" is evidence of this numbness. This activity produces only competitive results, a weak substitute for a heightened experience of life. Whatever physical changes are produced by competitive acts are more transient and leave us even more disconnected from an awareness of our current state than we were when we started.

In the context of physical challenges, the heightened experience I am referring to is the abiding sense of life, like the answer to the question, "Are you happy?" This is different from the temporary experience of any single event. No one would say that the sensation of a demanding physical challenge is a heightened experience, but it contributes to the abiding one that remains long after that challenge and changes us permanently. As you have likely figured out, competition does the opposite.

You Already Know What To Do

Because of my background, people often ask me for advice on matters of exercise. In most cases, the best response I can offer is to tell them to come back and ask me again only after they are convinced they are currently doing everything they already know to do. I have never had anyone ask me twice.

People have a couple of possible reasons for not returning. One is that they think I'm a jerk and was just dodging the question. (I hope that's not most people, but it's probably a few.) The second possibility is that my response compelled them to face the fact that they had been avoiding acting on the answers they already knew. Some, if not all, of those answers undoubtedly came from their own innate voice of wisdom. If I had answered any differently, I would just be adding to the library of answers that they would never actually act on.

You do know. And if you just imagine for a moment that you do know, the answer will come. Even if the first answer is not the perfect one, it will move you strongly in the right direction. It will evolve into the perfect choice(s) in short order and in the absence of experts, knowledge, rules saying "eat this, don't eat that," and step-by-step programs. None of that is necessary.

Other examples of this selective attention to our lives are found in those who work excessively on their careers and destroy important relationships in the process, or who sacrifice their physical health in the pursuit of mastering some technical skill. This picking and choosing doesn't work here, or anywhere, in your life. All of life is meant to be experienced just as it is and just as it is not.

Try as we might to use rules and ideas and specific instructions for the creation and maintenance of life as it was meant to be lived, we will fall short when any thing or person but nature is calling the shots. We will simply never shore up all the deficiencies that have been created by the modern (read: human-altered and sanitized) environment we have chosen for ourselves.

My purpose is not to suggest you should forevermore sleep on the ground and hunt your food. My goal is to simply reveal the folly of the attitude that modern life is a wholesale improvement, when clearly it is not. No matter how intelligent and carefully arranged our modern lives are, including those tidy and convenient gym hours, we will inevitably fail in the expression of wisdom that nature once brought to the process of creating a high quality of life.

One of the attitudes that created the mess we're in now regarding our physical state and the maintenance of it is the belief that our current practices are "just as good as" what humans have always done. If that were true, we would be as capable as early humans were of enduring life without any modern conveniences or comforts. How many of us would dare claim we could pass that test?

Accidental Fitness

Want six-pack abs? No problem; in fact, it's one of the simplest of all cosmetic accomplishments. But…really? Want a fulfilled life that leaves a legacy and makes a difference to those you love? Again, easily done. Except you can't have both. Those two accomplishments were carefully chosen to contrast with one another because they are mutually exclusive and come from two entirely different mindsets.

Do those six-pack abs serve any other purpose in life but recognition? A fulfilled life is really known by only one person: you. But the impact of that life is always felt by many others as the inevitable contribution you will make to the world.

If you still feel that you know what optimal fitness is, here's an easy test: Ask yourself again at precisely what quantifiable point a person crosses the line from unfit to fit. At precisely what quantifiable point does someone cross the line from unhealthy to healthy? At precisely what quantifiable point does someone cross the line from a destructive to a constructive diet?

Unless you can answer those questions coherently and without hesitation, you simply should not be using the words fit, healthy, or proper diet in conversation, ever. Likewise, you might think twice about purchasing or promoting products or practices that claim to provide one or all of those qualities. To do so, without an understanding of the limits of those values, means you will inevitably get it wrong and mislead yourself and (probably) waste your money in the process.

Forevermore, you will know that any news story or scientific article labeling exercise as "effective" means that it is not about vitality, functional capacity, longevity, or any other version of health that is purely personal. Instead, it will always be about the observable cosmetic or performance values that serve the logical version of our physical selves.

The bottom line is this: If it goes by any name other than honoring your life, it is wholly unnecessary to the fulfillment of why you're here. When you know that, the pursuit of something called fitness is a distraction from the goal, and it is a distraction from what we all can contribute to this world and the people in it because of who we are. Far from noble, modern-day fitness is a tremendously self-centered pursuit.

One inescapable fact is that your so-called fit body is destined to die with you. Or to some degree, it may die even sooner. However, your contribution to the world will live on as a legacy of your spirit and the way you chose to spend your time.

Perhaps this says it best: Humans never use the word fitness when talking about a child under the age of 10; we never use the word health when talking about ourselves until we're in our 30s; we never again use the word fitness when talking about ourselves after the age of 50; and we never use either word after the age of 80.

Have you ever wondered why we use them at only certain times of life? Or better still, does it make you wonder why we use those words at all?

FIVE
Phantom:Diet/Weight Loss

Key Message:
There is no need for a diet once you understand fitness.
There is no need for fitness once you understand health.
And there is no need for health once you understand life.

A key message of Aliveness is this: When it comes to behaviors and choices in life, it is not so much what you do that matters but why you do it. Even practices that can be clinically justified as constructive can quickly become destructive when the *why* is anything other than honoring life. Even purely physical (external) matters have value only relative to how they support a person's internal experience. Failing that, we're just marking time instead of living.

The why of most all popular practices labeled health, fitness, and diet are correctness and recognition, along with a few other standards and expectations that all originate somewhere outside ourselves. When the goal is measured in numbers, that is a clue that the only possible results are not about you or your life but instead just more data for comparison and debate. The number on the bathroom scale, a count of calories consumed, and a particular clothing size are great examples.

When you take an Aliveness approach to food, it starts

with simplification; refusing to overthink the subject. Even calling what you choose to eat a "diet" is an indication of this overthinking. Merely naming it indicates that you've already parsed food out from your experience of life as a whole. That requires thought, and thought is where trouble begins.

As with fitness and health, when you think of your nutrition as something separate and apart from your overall experience of life, you lose touch with the natural mechanism for guidance. In Aliveness, that guidance is always the quality of your experience, in the moment and in the long term. When that connection is broken by this act of naming, parsing and analysis, your next question will likely be, "Who can I ask about the right way to do this?"

But when food choices are guided by the quality of your experience, you will always do what makes your life better. In Aliveness, "overweight" is determined only by some negative effects on your experience, not the number on the bathroom scale. Those who carry noncontributory body fat never feel great and can never engage in all the activities they want to in support of their purpose. But they already know that, they already know why, and they already know what to do about it. That is experiential guidance at work.

Why Food Is Hard

As with so many other things in the realm of the physical world, eating constructively is hard because we have been told it is hard by people with something for sale, not because it is hard. In every practical way it is nothing more than another choice.

As with both health and fitness, the very best place to look for nutritional principles is in the behaviors of historic humans. Early humans had no choice but to eat what was available, when it was available, and in the amount that was available. In early times, that availability always worked out to be organic, local, seasonal, and less than we wanted but still enough.

As I've said before, people didn't always like that plan, but it always ensured a powerful combination of both quality and quantity that provided for a vital participation in life. This is evidence that the only diet you want is the one that people ate when they had no say in the matter. That turns out to also be the diet that sustained the species for thousands of years, through every imaginable hardship. Everything else is just a theory. The actual results (survival and thriving) of a process that spanned thousands of years constitutes one of the greatest scientific studies of all time, yet how quickly we dismiss it as antiquated and impractical. We're so sure we can do better.

So, what can we say about all these "new and improved" theoretical diets. Have they eliminated obesity, malnutrition, and degenerative diseases? Those conditions are on the rise most everywhere you look. Just calling it a plan and discussing its merits as a single source of guidance instantly makes it something less than ideal. Plus, you'll notice that those are quickly labeled by nutritionists as unsustainable and inconvenient, or they didn't provide rapid enough weight loss.

In modern times, though, we have willfully removed ourselves from the dictates of nature and corrupted our environment. Nowhere is that corruption more evident than in the average grocery store. Modern-day humans treat the local big-box grocery store as the arbiter of all-things-food. In other words, the subconscious belief is that everything in a grocery store is "food", and a secondary consideration is getting that food for as little money as possible. That's pretty much the extent of the thinking about food that many practice in modern times.

If we ever think beyond that, the next consideration is likely to be convenience. Hence, the quickie-mart and drive-through fast food. Finally, there is the very modern belief that some of our food can be categorized as a "treat," meaning only that we should just eat less of it.

All this thinking violates historical cues. Even so, because the grocery business has seemingly established (according to this common thinking) the baseline for what is food, most people will then proceed to defend this catalog as the universe of "normal" human nutrition.

If you were to follow the edicts of nature and subject food in its original form to minimal preparation, you would already raise the nutritional content of your food and its contribution to your life without even understanding how or why. These are all historical cues and about as simple as it comes. Sounds good and is good, at least compared with the average citizen's approach to nutrition.

But the benefits go up from there, depending on how consistent and sensitive you are to wisdom and nature. For example, nature would never give you an option to pick the evening's food based on "what sounds good tonight." The vast majority of diet plans created by today's experts would, by contrast, almost always approve—and even recommend—that as a reasonable consideration.

People make many similar errors in the modern notion of what to eat, even with the best of intentions. The one thing you can count on is that whoever promotes a diet on the basis of it being "correct" or "healthy" does not and cannot know how that diet affects *your* life. There is no universally correct or healthy experience when it comes to your life; only you can know what is or isn't right for you.

But human life is resilient and forgiving, and it takes a keen awareness of how you're feeling moment-to-moment to pick up on those internal cues. That's why the historical model of local, seasonal, organic, and less than you want is an excellent starting point.

How exactly, and to what extent, will you benefit from nature's plan as opposed to the diets established by today's experts? That is not really the point. Historical cues are not a diet, they are sensitivity training. Historical cues are not designed to produce perfect nutrition; even for you as an individual. The reason I referred to them as a "starting point" is because they are designed to wake up your body and your awareness to what elevates your experience. That awareness is what takes you the rest of the way.

After years of nutritional counseling as part of my fitness coaching practice, I can safely say that entering into "eat this, don't eat that" debates is a futile exercise. To counsel people who have accepted the grocery store paradigm as a sanctioned menu means you must begin by pointing out what they *should not* be eating. That kind of advice is usually met with howls of protest about being denied their "favorite" foods.

As a part of this resistance to change, big-box gatherers will demand some scientific proof for denying themselves the foods they like. This makes for a great avoidance strategy because most people know that science, no matter how established its declarations, is just the starting point for debate. And, as long as they can drag out the debate they don't actually have to act on it. As I said earlier, "don't eat that" debates are futile and never ending.

There will always be some version of science that says anything you can name is okay to eat (at least sometimes), and there will be other versions of science that say the same thing is *not* okay. The contradictions are not always in the science itself, but rather in differing interpretations of the very same science.

Whether contradictory conclusions are a part of the science itself or just the interpretations of the science, we nonscientists will never know, nor should we care. All we ever really know is someone's interpretation of the science anyway.

Faced with all of this contradictory science, many will simply throw up their hands and say, "To hell with it. I'm just gonna eat whatever I want because nobody's got the answer anyway." Who can blame them? Yet, that solution clearly doesn't work either because we have evidence of bodies failing from malnutrition (the prefix "mal" simply means corrupted), and that evidence is clear proof that something isn't working.

The problem here is not "eat this, don't eat that", the real problem is the common definition of food. Rather than demanding a reason not to eat something, let's come at it from the other direction by redefining the word "food." Since most of us have accepted a definition of food that includes everything available to us from the usual sources, let's start with a new foundation.

The starting point for this new foundation is the notion that *nothing is food*. From there, before we eat anything, we will need to be convinced, preferably by personal experience or some basic and time-honored principles, that it is constructive to the goal of our life. In other words, if we don't understand why we should eat something, then we don't eat it. One reason why we should eat something is that the substance in question has been around in its original form since the time of early humans; hence, local, seasonal, and organic.

Here is one of my favorite ways to think about that "what

is food?" question:

Food is that which is in its natural, unprocessed form and was typically available and reasonable to eat 5,000 or more years ago.

I am not a fan of anything called a "rule" when it comes to food. The above guidance is, instead, an expression of simple wisdom. It suggests that we choose only food that meets the criteria of seasonal, organic, and local, among other quality markers, without actually having to remember the details.

(The 5,000-year marker is mostly arbitrary and meant to indicate the time before agriculture became widespread. I realize that agriculture was practiced as early as 8,000 years ago, but routine hunting and gathering were still a major source of nutrition until approximately 5,000 years ago. That is the only significance of that time.)

"In its natural form" indicates that there should be no processing or adulteration in the preparation of the food other than heat, and it automatically eliminates anything in a package or a can.

"Reasonable to eat" means everything else you may need to know about food choices will be dictated by availability, simple common sense, and a desire to thrive.

For those who claim that they don't know what was typically available 5,000 years ago, making an intelligent best-guess will be a remarkably better approach than using this excuse to dismiss the principle. As I said earlier, historic cues aren't meant to be a diet per se. Rather, using them as a source of guidance is sensitivity training for waking up your own instinctual guidance. Another lesson in that sensitivity training is to honor the time in our history before profit-driven agriculture and "certified nutritional experts."

That takes the typical attitude about food and turns it on its head. Only then can we approach eating with the only understanding for which we have first-hand proof. The only good nonscientific reason that I can think of to eat something is that it promotes a supreme sense of vitality and presence in the world. This isn't an instant gratification, but it doesn't take as long as you may think.

With that reason as a new baseline, suddenly everything in the typical grocery store becomes suspect, as it should be. We're left with a very few items that can be identified as being in their true, unprocessed, and historical form. Then, we would put the same effort into demanding reasons that we should add other items, but that would be evidence in addition to that first test, not in place of it.

Aliveness Weight Loss

If I were coaching someone today about weight loss, my focus would be entirely on the quality of their internal life. Not the life that can be observed on the outside and described in language (like body fat), but the life of their experience.

No one suffers from a body composition that impacts their ability to enjoy life unless they are living with a corrupted experience. One of the symptoms of that corrupted experience is that it leaves us numb to the cues that would alert us to correct something in our life before that impact was problematic.

Therefore, I would never discuss food or exercise as a starting point for any physical state that is cause for concern. Neither food or exercise is the solution for that corrupted state. There may be a few theories to discuss somewhere down the line, but the only effective place to begin is by identifying it as a body composition that is the result of being out of balance with the design of life.

I would also never discuss it by using the word "weight". I used the phrase "weight loss" in the sub-heading above because it is the universally recognized name for a problem that frankly has nothing to do with body weight. As we have already discussed in regard to health and fitness, there is no standard for body weight that indicates a quality of life other than the experience of it. That experience is known by no one except you. The better you believe you can feel about life the more in line your body composition will be with the human design.

The composition of the body that provides for a vital life is always composed of lean muscle, water, blood, bones, connective tissues, organs, body fat, and the skin covering our bodies. But there is not now, nor has there ever been, a formula for the weight of each of those that provides for a maximum quality of life. We focus on body fat only because it can be seen and manipulated. But towards what end?

We all have body fat. How much body fat we carry translates into an experience of that weight. In other words, how it affects our enjoyment of life. That is the only relevant fact about body fat that we should be concerning ourselves with. But we should be concerned with that, except it seems that we're not. Instead, we're concerned with how we look, the number on the bathroom scale, and how we will be judged by others.

If our experience of life is suffering due to excess body fat, it is always and only because we have lost touch with the quality of our experience for a length of time that allowed that body fat to accumulate. In other words, we became distracted from caring for our lives. Losing touch with our experience is where the problem lies, not in any form of ignorance or misunderstanding about food.

In my fitness practice my approach to weight loss was the typical one of sitting down with clients and talking about food choices. I had lots to share, but I eventually realized that the point of those consultations was not weight loss; those clients could have chosen from a thousand established and widely known schemes to accomplish that. The real point was the hope that I would provide a new scheme that didn't require big changes in their current and comfortable lifestyle. Since their lifestyle *was the problem*, that wasn't likely to happen with me. Part of the lifestyle that they didn't want to address was the persistent quality of life, and the emotional struggles they were experiencing. Yet, that is always the root of the issue.

I'm sure you've heard many reports from those who have allowed their body composition to become corrupted about how they got that way. It is a near-universal story of using food as a substitute for their emotional needs. But have you ever heard even one report of someone saying they just didn't know enough to stay lean? Rhetorical question; I already know the answer.

Outside of acute and diagnosable conditions, the only reason anyone consults with fitness experts, nutritionists, or dieticians about weight loss is in an attempt to skirt the real cause and wanting instead to just correct the symptoms. Those experts don't know how you feel, they only know how you look along with a few numbers for the chart. Most aren't engaged in any act of deceit, they truly believe it is a clinical problem with a clinical solution.

So, let's clear this up right now: The number of people who become obese due entirely to a lack of information is zero. It is always a matter of becoming detached from our internal guidance; which is just another way of saying that we currently feel bad about life.

Yet, we insist on treating it with "new, improved, miracle of science" diets and scientific studies and by-the-numbers food plans and "struggling with weight" victimization. I hope this book will in some small way change the conversation about health, fitness, and weight loss so that we stop throwing money at fitness experts and dieticians in our attempt to avoid doing what we already know. Hopefully, one day, all of this nonsense about calories and bathroom scales and "eat this, don't eat that" can be tossed on the scrapheap of other long-forgotten misguided thinking.

We already know that whatever cosmetic improvements we realize from "breakthrough discoveries" and regimented food plans—if they produce change at all—are ultimately temporary and superficial fixes. The cases of those who have lost significant weight are heralded as success stories despite the fact that the vast majority of them regain the weight at some future point. Now you know why.

Those who I consulted recognized their excess body fat, and wanted to be lean, but any prescribed regimen for eating was guaranteed to clash with the defenses they had already built up around food. I had people stand up and walk out on diet conversations because I refused to endorse the way they were already eating. There were others who I suspected were just too polite to actually walk out, but had no intention of taking my advice.

The plain fact is that most people in need of dropping body fat are not doing what they already know they need to do. Clearly whatever information I could offer, no matter how statistically effective and scientifically proven it may be, wasn't going to fare much better.

Likewise, there are many who sense internally that they want to create a leaner body composition for the sake of honoring their life apart from any appearance concerns. Those folks will accomplish that goal with little or no input from any professional or expert on the subject. Once you make the quality of your own experience the goal, there is wisdom available to you that might not have been available with any other intent.

Human defenses around food are as volatile as defenses around religion. This is the same dogma we discussed in the last chapter around various fitness practices. Dogma is only present when we submit to external voices on a subject rather than acknowledging our own inner guidance. Those external voices have their own agenda, and that agenda is never the quality of *your* life. It is usually money, but it may also be positioning for some form of control over others.

The bottom line of all of this though is still the personal experience of it. What always drives us to seek some goal other than feeling good about life is the perception that there is some imminent threat which must be dealt with first. Feeling unsafe is the only thing that will draw your awareness away from how you feel inside your body. The only possible path to extricating yourself from dogma—whether the subject is food, religion, politics, whatever—is to recognize how all of this logic and ideology makes you feel. It isn't good.

Nutritionists and registered dieticians will always protect their pocketbook first. The same is true for health and fitness coaches. This is not to single out and demean these categories of people though because protecting the pocketbook has overtaken honoring life as the Prime Directive of our society. Under this Directive, the quality of your life—internal or external—will always take a back seat to how much you are willing to pay.

Scientific studies and food plans and exercise programs and "miracle breakthrough" potions and 4-color handouts all serve to improve the perceived value and exclusivity of their information. And it doesn't really tax anyone's capacity for discernment to see that convincing you to distrust your own wisdom as a source of guidance works out very well for their income stream.

I will leave you to determine to exactly what degree this fact is corrupting the advice, but to say that it is irrelevant would be an obvious example of denial. In their defense I doubt that many of them are even aware that this is the mission. Profiteering is so ingrained in our culture as to be invisible especially to those who are benefitting the most from it. We would all do well to remember that the profit motive is the single most destructive influence on the integrity of life; human and otherwise.

A better experience of life is a better life, regardless of how it looks to anyone else or how scientifically justifiable it is. If you had no internal guidance, science would be the best guidance there is. But you do. We will always know we are on the right path in the recognition of an improving experience of life, not by correctly implementing the latest verdict of science.

This internal sense is constantly providing guidance about the choices that cause your life to thrive. Never doubt that wisdom is available to each and every one of us. But, it also goes about its work quietly and with zero fanfare, which means it is all too easy to ignore; especially when the promoters of "things for sale" have turned the volume of their messages up to 11.

None of that noise is about you except by coincidence. Yet, wisdom is *only* about you. Whatever else you do to address concerns about nutrition and body fat, make sure that it comes only after you have exhausted the advice from your own internal wisdom first.

Even with this guidance, there is tremendous latitude in the food choices that can produce the goal of Aliveness. And the actual choices that produce that outcome for you are most likely going to be different from those of nearly every other person with the same goal.

That is why, to whatever extent we choose to talk about nutrition, I never refer to it as a diet, but rather as an individual "foodstyle." A foodstyle is a pattern and governance to eating that applies only to you, requires no justification or approval of science, and benefits only you. The only absolute in that plan is that it elevates your experience of life.

Nothing said here about appropriate human nutrition is meant to be a replacement for a simple and powerful awareness of the only truth about your life that there will ever be: how you feel as a result of what you eat. Most of us think of "presence" as a mental gimmick to promote calm and clarity of thinking, and it is that. But it doesn't stop there. It extends to a far greater awareness of how things like nutrition affect our lives moment to moment, not just the next time we get on the scale.

Just Stop Talking

Remember that, in the entire history of the species, until very recent times, people have never had to think much about food. There is no justification for the use of the word "healthy" or "correct" when referring to food. There are huge and obvious flaws with every standard used to justify these assertions. The most common standard, of course, is weight loss.

What is your first thought when you look at the number

on that bathroom scale? If you're human, that number automatically puts you in a judgmental (read: non-present) frame of mind. That's what numbers do. Calories are another example. When that logical mindset is turned on things never end well for your humanity. That number on the scale doesn't care about your life any more than the lottery numbers you picked care how much you need the money.

Have you ever wondered why we treat being underweight as a psychological condition, but we treat being overweight as a physical one when, in fact, they are both symptoms of the same thing? Other common misunderstandings about weight loss have to do with the language used to discuss it. In the business of weight loss, it is often said that people "struggle" with weight loss, or they are "fighting" excess weight. This paints a picture of you as a victim of non-constructive pounds waiting around every corner to attach themselves to your body through no fault of your own.

Non-constructive body weight is always the result of behaviors that are not about Aliveness. No one "struggles" or "fights" something that they are also causing. There is no "struggle" in the desire to be more alive other than departing from familiar routines that keep you from it. But just as we created the routine to begin with, we can create a new one that maximizes our experience of life first. Convincing you that you are in a "fight" is the entrée to offering you something for sale that will be your ally in the battle.

Here is evidence that we no longer practice Aliveness or even know it's a thing: The next time you see an article about diets—specifically, one that rates the "quality" of diets—notice the standard by which that quality is judged. Inevitably, diets are judged solely on their ability to produce the highest rate and degree of weight loss. They may also add other qualifiers like "sustainable," but I've never seen a study that tracks respondents for any length of time to determine that.

If weight loss were all that mattered, the highest rate and degree of that result is always achieved when people eat no food at all. That's the absurdity of using weight loss as the primary indicator of anything having to do with the quality of your food. If you are overweight, you are malnourished and don't feel good. If you are underweight, you are also malnourished and don't feel good. The common theme is always "don't feel good".

When you treat weight loss as an absolute standard for the specifics of a food plan, you inadvertently support the condition known as anorexia. An anorexic is simply someone who accepts the absolute goal of weight loss as positive, literally and without standards, which is exactly what the business of weight loss programs and pills need you to believe. Without that belief, they would have no business.

This is not a life-affirming way to live. Yet, it is all perfectly acceptable in the modern paradigm of for-profit health and nutrition. In fact, it is the only common thread through every Conversation on the subject of "healthy eating."

When we cease to view these dietary strategies as absolutes, we will eliminate the need for the labels that now go with them, and the debate over the specifics. That, of course, leaves the enterprising sorts with nothing to sell, so the entire weight loss industry will quickly collapse under its own weight (see what I did there?) were this ever to be a widely embraced understanding.

Can you imagine people of 5,000 years ago sitting around discussing the merits of their food choices? Like debates about health or fitness among people of that time, this idea would be laughable. Nature's realities would make that a very short discussion. Now, we want to talk about dietary choices endlessly and debate the results of various scientific studies that tell us this is bad and that is good.

Also, have you noticed how every new diet that acquires a name like "Atkins", "South Beach", "Mediterranean", etc. quickly attracts the label of "fad"? Once the book about any new diet is published and the websites begin to emerge, the dieticians and nutritionists all want to be the first to tell you everything that is bad about the new plan. This has never not been true, and it says so much more about our fascination with the "game" of nutrition. Namely, all a nutritionist must do to appear superior to those who develop new diets is to be a critic of them. Where is the benefit to those of us simply looking for better nutrition?

What if, instead, we all just stopped talking about food and, especially, stopped calling our foodstyle by a name. Then, what if our only plan was to be happy with who we are, how we are, and where we are in life. The wisdom revealed in this plan would inevitably lead us to also eat local, seasonal, organic, and less than we want, but that's where the debate would end.

Can you imagine how much more vital we would be? With those simple principles there would be no obesity, no abnormal degeneration, and far fewer of the other ailments that are connected to modern life. The only real danger in this is that our brains would take over once again and give this plan a name.

Leave the debate, the diet naming, and the scientific studies to the dieticians and nutritionists. Your time and other resources are best spent working on honoring your life. If that is all you ever did, you'd be closer to a foodstyle that supports a fulfilled life than anyone who is just after more "healthy points." A foodstyle that supports your purpose in life will never be the clinically correct one.

Are there things you just shouldn't eat? Of course. Everything that was unavailable 5,000 years ago should be subjected to extreme scrutiny, mostly by you. The only guiding principle that is true for you is how your nutrition supports your purpose in life and, correspondingly, how it affects your experience moment to moment. Whatever else may be true about nutrition, the way you feel is truer.

There is no need for a diet once you understand fitness. There is no need for fitness once you understand health. And there is no need for health once you understand life.

SIX
For Scientists Only

Key Message:
Good science is always right, or as right as right can be, and good science is still the wrong tool for creating satisfaction with life.

The chapter is falsely titled "For Scientists Only" to make a point. Thank you for ignoring it and reading anyway.

The point is about the folly of lay persons pretending that they understand science. That folly is one of the reasons so many of us can be persuaded to treat relatively trivial or irrelevant concepts as important to life and happiness because of *the science*. Even the word "science" is assumed to carry so much weight in the Conversation that we believe "knowing the science" behind a product or practice is essential to determining the value of it. We believe that if science has studied it, it must be important. In the realm of life experience, this is never true.

A practical summary of the value of science is this: "Science is the most trustworthy source of information we have in all clinical matters." "Clinical matters" are those that can be measured and will provide adequate data for a logical analysis to either prove or disprove a theory. The reason this process holds little hope of helping us live more fulfilled lives is that the experience of human life—that which we all seek, and the subject of this book—is not a clinical matter. The ultimate experience of a human can never be found in quantification, data, or analysis; in fact, to do so will subvert the cause and the experience of our humanity.

Science is a distinctly logical construct. It is the very expression of logical processes and one of the legitimate uses for it. But just like logic itself, science has limitations in its application and is prone to misuse, not by some flaw in the process, but by a flaw in human nature. The flaw is our belief that the qualities of human life can be found by the processes of logic.

An easily relatable way to understand logic is to think of it as the process by which we determine what *most likely is*. It requires, first, a problem to solve and then a theory about what should be the solution. Next is a gathering of data relevant to the theory. After that comes an analysis of the data as a test of that theory. From this analysis, we either prove or disprove the theory to the best of our ability.

But then, even if it is validated by the scientific process, it is still only rightfully identified as something that *should be,* not *that is*. Not even the longest-standing scientific conclusions can be called absolute truth. They are still just the theories that have yet to be disproven, like the theory of gravity, for example. And, until they are disproven they are the safest of all bets.

Sounds good so far. So, what is a misuse of this process? Do you really want to know the science behind why you love a piece of music or another person? You're too busy enjoying the experience of love to care much about the why of it. The time spent analyzing it will be time spent not enjoying it. Yet that is what many do and consider to be the "smart" way to proceed in life.

But realize that most of us identify what most likely is based on other people's opinions that we treat as legitimate "data." Think for a moment about how often you use the word "should" in conversation and self-talk on a subject that is unique to you and your choices. Since what *should be* isn't *what is* about you, it must be arrived at by some process other than how it feels. That process always involves giving absolute authority to someone else's opinion.

Science is very good at what it does, but few of us really understand what it does. According to the famed psychologist Abraham Maslow, a scientist himself, even scientists don't understand what science does or how to get the most from it. And it is in no case an absolute arbiter of truth and fact. Science is true only to the extent that it is a fact that has yet to be disproven, despite people's rigorous attempts to do so.

It's easy to spot the connection between "should" and "science." Since the conclusions of science are what *should be*, based on all available evidence, it is only in the experiences of life *that are*—like happiness, fun, creativity, and other wholly unreasonable pursuits—that I dismiss science as a constructive source for guidance. I am not anti-science in any other sense. I am anti-science only when science is being used by nonscientists and for the nonclinical matter of experience.

The scientific version of love (the purest form of experience), for example, is making a list of pros and cons as a way to decide if you should marry someone. This is a classic misapplication of logic, treating love as a clinical matter rather than a human choice. It is only those who have given the experience of their life over entirely to logic who believe these lists are a good idea.

Isn't it actually the mystery and unreasonableness of love that we cherish the most? Would you really want the choice of whom to love be the result of scientific analysis or a computer algorithm? That is the moment it would instantly cease to be love and become a clinical matter producing a logical conclusion.

I study the science of psychology and have for most of my life. But we all know that psychology doesn't have all the answers for a quality experience of life. If it did science would have eradicated unhappiness just as it did polio. Yet I also know that I am capable of being happy by my own devices and at any moment. De facto that means, for my life and my life only, I know something that science does not. The same is true for you. And the same is true in other realms of science, but only in its ability to enhance the experience of your own life. Fortunately, the experience of your own life is the subject of this book.

If you are not confusing safety for happiness, you can always know that your own satisfaction with life may benefit from science in some ways, but the last word is yours and yours alone.

I have formed many experience-based conclusions about my own life that have helped me immensely, but then I encounter someone who claims science has a better way. The typical response would be to embrace the science because *it's science*, and to ignore the fact that it fails to accomplish the only thing that really matters.

The overreliance on science to answer a question of life is driven by the human need for certainty. A certain future is one example of an absolute arbiter of fact and truth, which is, in turn, a byproduct of neurological (perceived) fear. That future is something that can be counted on to never lie to us, to never steer us wrong, and to never cause us to spin our wheels or waste our time in our quest for guidance toward a safer life. Despite all that it is likely not the best future available to us.

The vast majority of us have chosen to allow science to guide us to that certain future even though it can only promise safety. Safety is the goal of logic, and the more we romanticize logic rather than respect it, the more we will continue to engage it to provide answers it was never designed to address. The Aliveness approach to logic is that it should only ever be scrutinized and tolerated, but never celebrated.

Looking at science in that way provides a much more realistic impression of its reliability in the search for a more fulfilled life. But our own innate wisdom regarding the important aspects of human life is far more reliable than science in that it gives the experience of life equal, if not exclusive, weight in the consideration. What wisdom is not is certain.

In any matter that affects the quality of our experience of life, our internal wisdom is the closest thing we have to a trustworthy arbiter of truth and fact because, in this realm, truth and fact are experiential and unique to each of us; there is very little commonality to a successful life.

For everything inside the realm of shared truth, like medicine or space travel, science is the very best source of guidance there is. For personal truth, it is quite useless. That is a crucial distinction, but it is a distinction far too few of us take into account. We have been told, and have come to believe, that science is the answer to the entirety of being human. It is stated as such in the Conversation at every turn, and too many of us act as if it were true.

In practice, an interpretation of science is all anyone can

know, except for those who actually engaged in the research and who are responsible for the conclusions drawn from that data. That is not you. It's not me, either. Although the mere presence of all of that scientific-sounding "data" probably impressed the socks off you, you were mostly impressed by the author's apparent ability to actually understand it because you certainly didn't. Being dutifully impressed by all those multisyllabic words and the assumption that whoever was presenting it understood it fully, you mostly became impressed with the writer, not the science.

The most important thing for you to know about this book is that it contains nothing that cannot be understood—and in turn, both practiced and taught—by the average 10-year-old. Children of that age can create higher levels of useful Aliveness than a research lab full of scientists and would do so naturally if adults and all their noble-sounding logical constructs didn't come along and screw it up for them.

I don't need you to believe that I am smart or unique, and I certainly don't need you to believe that I have any "secret" information or "astounding new breakthroughs" to share. Rather, I am here only to show you that it doesn't take a smart person to comprehend or teach Aliveness, and I do not pretend to have all the answers you seek because the questions are unique to you and the answers are yours alone to discover.

The truth about all of those smart scientists and gurus, and their answers, is this: the human body is astoundingly complex and it is fully understood by no one. The best any of us can hope for in the search for a thriving body is to learn the behaviors by which we can coax the greatest degree of Aliveness out of ourselves. The physical state created by Aliveness can and must be about results, not theories or great-sounding notions that you will never fully understand; it must be based on just profound and experiential results instead of debate. Debate is the alternative to understanding.

When you apply that simple understanding to your own life, some amazing things start to happen. You become a model of personal presence to your family, community, and humans everywhere. You stand up straighter, you speak with more authority, you get more done, you have more and better relationships, and you laugh more. These are the results I'm talking about. And the results that create a fulfilled human.

In the realm of physical robustness, the only thing you might not know is how to counteract the inevitable effects of modern life. Modern life itself is a destructive influence on your wellbeing because it is largely a product of logic. As such, it is both foreign and artificial. Although you cannot escape all of those destructive effects, the best defense is still your choices about how and where to spend your time that minimize the "modern" and maximize the "life".

With any matter that affects the quality of our experience, our internal wisdom is the closest thing we have to a trustworthy arbiter of personal truth and fact. To the matter of human life, truth and fact are unique to each of us and are guided by what feels best; there is little universality to the quality of a life.

Here is one of those fine lines where a willingness to be guided by wisdom rather than data makes a huge difference in the outcome: the distinction between physical healing and the prevention of that which requires healing. Prevention is purely empirical and experiential. Healing is purely theoretical.

The scientific version of guidance for our lives probably sounds like a perfectly reasonable process for making decisions that will move our lives along, and it will accomplish some degree of that. But to pursue that you must ignore the fact that it is loaded with limitation and uniformity. Neither of those feels good on the inside. In the scientific version of life, the highest priority is placed on being viewed as "normal" and "correct," not fulfilled or happy. This is always a trade-off between a life of energized satisfaction and one of certainty and facts.

Data is only a report on what already is and has been, what is reasonable, and what is probable. If that doesn't sound much like a life bound for greatness, that's because it's not. Nothing you would ever describe as exceptional or great has ever been created by that process. It is, instead, the process for conformity.

Here's another way to view it: What does it mean to be correct? If you are faced with two choices, one that has the backing of critical analysis, widespread public opinion, and/or experts, and one that produces an obviously better experience of your life, which would you choose? Is it difficult for you to step away from the data and the support of your social circle long enough to consider another path that only your internal wisdom tells you is a better one? Even if only for you?

Nothing exceptional in the world was ever created unless someone made just that choice. That's a strong indication of the influence that critical analysis has over our lives. So the real question is, "Do you want to have a correct life by a universal standard, or a happier life by a personal standard?" It's quite an upset to most people to learn that those are almost never the same thing.

Critical analysis produces theories about the subject of the data. Theories are about only what has been in the past and what probably will be for the future based on the data from the past. Theories are never about possibility, potential, and creation. Can you see how much of life is missing from the theories about it? Yet this is what we settle for when we identify with our capacity for logic in the realms of health, fitness, and weight loss.

Logic fools us because it all sounds so true. Here you have one of the greatest distinctions between experience and analysis: universally true vs. personally true. To understand this distinction, you need an accurate definition of "true." The only truth humans ever know is the personal experience of their own life. There is no other truth, only analysis, conjecture, theory, speculation, and opinion. We try to find some satisfaction with life in those things, but they will only ever appeal to our brain's capacity for correctness.

If you feel that you don't have enough experience with something to know how it feels to you, what is still available is called a choice. Whereas critical analysis demands a correct answer, with a choice, there is no such thing. There is every possibility for each choice and never a fear of getting it wrong. As I said, choosing is no more serious an act than picking a flavor of ice cream. Much of life is determined by simple choices, and success in life is possible only when we are comfortable with the uncertainty of our own choices.

If your highest goal in the moment is to heal from some known physical condition or acute symptom, that is where I strongly recommend that you see a doctor or other medical professional. Those are situations where science will serve you best. This is the proper application of science.

However, a slavish reliance on scientific justification of strategies for improving the quality of your life is actually a form of experiential laziness. We are substituting an act of awareness and trust in our own wisdom with new information. All the most beautiful experiences in life defy scientific justification. Creativity, art, and intimate relations are some examples. Since we are always free to choose that to which we apply logic, we can and often do make decisions instead of choices. And decisions don't care about the quality of our experience; only choices do that.

No matter how much we profess to love and depend on science for all matters of health and fitness, we all choose to circumvent it on occasion if the science doesn't mesh with the intent. A prime example is how we often ignore medical advice. You've seen this when there's a prize involved like a trophy for some athletic competition. Or, when a personal goal demands we use our bodies in unnatural ways, like running a marathon or seeking drastically low levels of body fat. Yet we treat those accomplishments as if, they too, were suggestive of health and fitness; we even call them by those names. To do so is a real stretch of any plausible definition for either word.

For the goal of a better life, the suggestion to source your guidance somewhere other than science is not as crazy as it may seem on the surface. You already do that very thing often and with no ill-effects. In fact, being guided by internal wisdom mostly results in the best of all possible outcomes. The reason you're not aware of it is because it is a purely natural act that requires no awareness or logic (thinking).

Remember again that the subject is the quality of your life; not the avoidance of imminent threats to survival. Threats are a great use of your logical brain, but they happen so rarely that you likely cannot even remember the last time you needed to deal with something that had the potential to end your life.

There is a source for everything that will contribute to you being wholly satisfied with your life in each moment. For that goal there is a real and profound well of guidance which we may all access and trust more than we do. It's called internal wisdom.

Will your internal wisdom ever lead you down a destructive path? That's the argument your brain throws out whenever you're tempted to seek guidance from an illogical source. To suggest that it will (or even could) be destructive is to lack an adequate understanding of, and experience with, that wisdom.

Wisdom is the only intelligence in the universe that cares about you as an individual. Remember that science is only shared knowledge about universal concerns. Once you make it about "shared" and "universal", there is not much left that is about you and your life.

You learn to identify and trust that personal wisdom through sensations in your body. Think of it this way: how do you know when you *want* or *like* something? There are only two sensations that lead you to seek some tangible thing or experience that you would call *wanting*. One is that you fear not having it. In other words, you believe the thing you want will make your life safer in the face of a hostile world. Or, two, imagining the experience of it causes a pleasant sensation in your body. The first is a fear response, which is another way of describing an *inauthentic want*. The second is allowing a sensation in your body to guide your choices.

It is that second one that describes the process of accessing your internal wisdom. Every stimulus including a thought causes a physical response in the body. Wisdom is simply interpreting that response as guidance. A simplified version of that guidance is this: when it's a positive response, move closer. When it's negative, move away.

You tap into it by eliminating information coming from

outside yourself. That is also the very thing that must happen for you to authentically answer the question, "what do you want?" or, "how are you?" If you cannot readily and confidently identify your own wisdom distinct from all other input, then you are still subject to being confused or misled, and will mostly be guided by logic.

Until you are convinced that you have that ready access and have developed a solid foundation of trust in your internal guidance, then science will be the best thing you have and I suggest you rely on it instead. But don't ever assume that it is also the best source of guidance you have.

Because you are not a scientist, your information is second hand. Any scientific conclusion that reaches you was filtered through someone—and probably several someones—on its way to you. Was there any interpretation, omission, flaw, or outright corruption contained in this filtered conclusion? In today's world, any of the above is not only possible but common. Therefore, unless you have personally spoken to the scientist(s) who actually conducted the study that led to the conclusion, your only choice is to treat that conclusion as an opinion, not fact; worthy of consideration, but not actionable without further scrutiny.

About anything having to do with your quality of life, when science suggests one course of action and your own wisdom is telling you something different, your choice becomes a very personal one. Of course you will inform yourself on what reliably-sourced science has to say (if there is any), but to become dogmatic about your choice is no more warranted than being dogmatic about your favorite flavor of ice cream. There will never be anything such as scientific truth about how you feel. Or, put another way, what ever else may be true, how you feel is truer.

My other chief concern about science is that the misuse of it by nonscientists is common practice by those with things for sale. Promoters of things for sale will claim scientific evidence for the efficacy of a product or practice where no legitimate science exists. Phony white papers and "summaries" of science (rather than the scientific study itself) supporting products and other theories are everywhere. This is why it is dangerous for nonscientists to pretend to rely on science when they are unable to determine if what they're hearing or reading is, in fact, science at all.

There is still a foundation, or basis, for guidance that is far more trustworthy and has stood the test of time since the dawn of our species; the time before science, scientists, and experts of all kinds. It is a foundation of experience. What makes a better experience is a better practice. This is non-theoretical. It is, in fact, empirical and an uncomfortable proposition only for those who have placed their trust in logic for guidance in what are experiential matters.

Good science is always right, or as right as right can be, and good science is still the wrong tool for creating satisfaction with life. Trusting science with the quality of your experience is like playing the piano with a hammer. The hammer is a great tool but wholly destructive to the task at hand. Science discovers the proof that something will work most of the time; experience bypasses the proof and skips right to results. Whatever science discovers will just confirm what the people who rely on internal wisdom have known for a long time.

The satisfaction with our lives that we all seek will never be found in a number or critical analysis. No matter what those things represent, the fact that they do not represent an experience means we have already missed the point of life.

Science does not love you. Science merely reports on data about you. Science does not and cannot know and comprehend you. Only you can do that for yourself.

Nevertheless, science is a wonderful thing. My only suggestion is that you do not wait for science before you act on behalf of your life. You have wisdom in you that no one else knows or can know. Science will always be in addition to that, not instead of it.

The title of this book describes the result of changing your external state through new practices or products before, or instead of, changing your internal state (how it feels to be you). If you are thinking about spending money on any program, product, pill, or diet with health or fitness as the promise, remember that there is no basis to make that claim because there is no definition for either one. What else aren't they telling you.

There is nothing about the next step in your search for a more fulfilled and satisfied life that you don't already know. The ego says that the problem is out there, never that the solution is in here. And, included in "out there" is your own body.

But your body is not a problem that needs fixing. It is merely a result of the stand you have taken in life. That stand is yours and yours alone, it requires no justification or validation, and it can be altered any time you would like to experience a different body.

SEVEN

Where's My Trophy?

Key Message:
Even though we often rail against divisiveness in polite society, our behaviors reveal that we love divisiveness when it is called "sports."

I've always found it interesting that some of us march out of adolescence into adulthood with the greatest confidence in, and respect for, that which makes us unique, while others are so easily seduced by logic's pursuit of competition and conformity. The latter path is easily identified in the pursuits of health, fitness, and regimented diets.

Is there some switch in childhood that gets flipped one way or the other? That question may strike you as facetious, but this chapter makes the case for just such a switch, and explains how it gets flipped in childhood through the indoctrination of our children and the modeling they do of those around them.

The misapplication of logic is the greatest single source of suffering and limitation in adults, and it is the cause of living specialized and unsatisfied lives. Parents and other influential adults have a huge impact on whether children will grow up to misuse and over-rely on logical constructs as adults.

As parents who want to see their children live full and successful lives, we will want to know what role we play in that. As adults with varying degrees of suffering caused by our own childhoods, we have access to a self-directed reparenting of ourselves, and we can learn much about that process from understanding how we got here. Essentially, this reparenting is an undoing of some specific and destructive influences from those early years. But how much better to avoid the need for that in the first place.

An over-reliance on logic may have began in childhood, but it is compounded when those children grow into adults and have children of their own. As adults, we are incapable of teaching a respect for life if we do not know the experience of that ourselves. The passing on of a parent's logic-centric approach to life, along with so many other life lessons, occurs unnoticed as adults who have lived with it all of their lives. By adulthood, they will perceive logic to be just another word for the real world.

Consider how often you hear adults use anecdotes from the world of sports used as metaphors for success in life. This sports-as-life corollary is trotted out by nearly every authority on self-help or personal development, and it is an accepted theme in promoting personal responsibility and teaching success in business.

Life coaches all have their litany of sports-as-business anecdotes that appear to prove the point that discipline, practice, and self-sacrifice are the keys to success of all kinds, including just being happy! That they call themselves "coaches" is a clue to their affinity for competitive practices. What is missed in this approach is that discipline, practice, and self-sacrifice are instead the cause of personal struggles, not the solution for them.

Even those of us who weren't raised in a logic-centric environment find it difficult to ignore logic's influence on the world. It is so pervasive as to make it difficult to have some relationships, do business, or even carry on a productive conversation without slipping into that mindset.

Yet, there are many who can still recognize the emotionless state that logic demands, and it doesn't feel good. That remains the one and only clue that our warm and colorful spirits have taken a backseat to the cold, black and white world of logic.

Have you ever automatically assumed principles of competition provide some relevance to personal fulfillment? This assumption is common because it is so pervasive and sounds so believable; it just seems so much like something that should be true. We accept what sounds true and should be true when it comes from supposedly credible sources and despite its conflict with our quality of life and internal wisdom. That is, once again, the story of The Emperor's New Clothes. That new suit of clothes is so believable because it is exactly what you would expect an emperor to be wearing.

The Parent Trap

I had occasion to mention in an earlier chapter a few of the subtler ways that logic shows up in our experience: things like comparison, a craving for information, orderliness, correctness, a dependence on rules and absolutes, the quantification of life (a dependence on numerical references), conformity, and the tendency to turn choices into decisions. But there are others, including an attraction to competition.

We won't easily connect the dots between logic and those

attitudes and beliefs because logic presents itself as reality of the highest degree, which means that these attitudes and beliefs will be perceived as correct and inevitable, and thus to challenge them would be foolish.

But we see logical constructs through a new lens when we choose to give greater weight to the obvious unreasonableness of life. Realize that I'm using "unreasonableness" as a virtue; virtues like emotion, humor, spontaneity, creativity, love, and presence; in short, a general sense of excitement about what life has in store for us. All will fail the test of logic but contribute greatly to the cause of life at the same time.

If we have fewer of those unreasonable but satisfying experiences than we want, we can be sure the cause is an over-reliance on logic to guide our lives. As time goes on, it gets easier to spot the symptoms of logic at work in our lives directly, but in the meantime we always know one thing: No matter what else in life we may or may not be aware of, when we identify a dearth of experiential qualities like emotions, creativity, love, humor, etc., we can also identify an excessive reliance on logic; in ourselves and our children.

How we end up in life is heavily influenced by how we start out. As adults, we see the world precisely as our parents did, with little deviation, generally speaking. Whether the world is a friend or an enemy is one of those deep-seated beliefs about life that is largely determined by the most influential people around us as children and the value they placed on logic.

One of the earliest and most common introductions to logic is the celebration of competition. Specifically, participation in, or even glorification of, competitive sports in kids who are encouraged by parents at an early age. Human-on-human competition is Logic 101.

If you are a parent, I'm going to go out on a limb and guess that you love your child. I'm also going to assume that you work every minute of every day at the task of being the best parent you can be. I want every parent to know that none of that is in question here. Although love may be all that is required to raise active and fulfilled children, the question becomes, what might you also be doing that is not love? That is, how might you instead be surreptitiously dismantling what love builds?

This chapter is not only a message to parents but also a message about what all of us likely experienced as children ourselves. The role that parents play in a child's development is no more mysterious than most believe; it is just differently mysterious. Turns out, the only role a parent needs to fill is that of being a model of a satisfied life.

Ideally, parents will exhibit a life that honors experience, anticipates the future, and merely tolerates logic as a tool. Whatever attitudes and beliefs parents possess are being modeled for their children every minute of every day. This model is informed by the very thoughts you think, the absent-minded words you say, and the life you choose to live.

I have mentioned that one of my specialties as a fitness coach was training athletes for competition. But what I haven't said is that many of these athletes were kids. Not only did I run a sports preparedness clinic for kids 11 to 16 years old who had athletic aspirations, I worked individually with some who already were fiercely competitive by 12 or 13.

I think we can all agree that we don't want our 12-and 13-year-old kids to be "fiercely" anything. But that's always the inevitable result of the spirit of competition. Not only were these kids strongly competitive, but that attitude was both encouraged and celebrated by their parents.

What I noticed about these kids was that they had largely lost that whimsical nature of childhood. There was little evidence of laughter and imagination; those were replaced by concentration, intensity, and judgment. In short, these kids were no longer much fun to be around. But their rapidly developing egos were being bolstered by a glorification of athletic competition at home and elsewhere.

Competition is a compelling concept to our capacity for logic, even that of a young child. The capacity develops slowly; very little of it is present in children under the age of two. In the realm of child development there is a phase known as the "terrible twos," when logic begins to assert itself and gradually grows from there into full bloom by age 12.

Despite the label of "terrible", it is actually just a different way of interpreting the world that is a clue about the destructive power of logic. It is engaged in its own form of competition with our intrinsic humanity.

To keep logic in perspective through childhood requires, first, that parents learn to distinguish between logic and humanity. Not only are they irretrievably distinct, these two forces are mutually exclusive values, pulling each of us in opposite directions in a battle for our awareness. The weight we give to each is one of the choices life asks us to make.

Then, to pass that distinction on to their kids and to always support choices that are guided by humanity (like love and compassion) and personal experience (like creation and imagination), and to merely tolerate the occasional and necessary dalliances with logic. In this way, parents provide subtle guidance about the influences that will serve the child better in their own personal aspirations, which always pays huge dividends down the road.

Logic Needs an Enemy

However, the corrupting power of logic isn't a cause for fear any more than the occasional need for logic is a cause for celebration. It's dangerous only when we can't distinguish between the two. Logic is constructive as a tool, but destructive as a source of guidance for our lives. But we can easily become persuaded that everything in life benefits from seeing it through the lens of logic. This is a virtue that it clearly does not deserve, but it is apparent in the fact that both children and adults glorify competition.

Some of the easiest money you'll ever make comes from selling something that you can claim is about winning a competition against another human. As the old saying goes, no one ever went broke appealing to a person's capacity for logic. The nobility it enjoys can be explained as a symptom of recognizing its enticements in the absence of any acknowledgement of its side effects. Every innovation looks great until you discover you can't afford it.

Professional sports always reminds me of the Roman Coliseum and fight-to-the-death contests between gladiators and lions. That sounds barbaric today but it's a short leap between that and what happens in many modern-day contests like MMA and boxing. We sow the seeds of that on every youth sports field. That would seem to be a fairly obvious connection but one we have ignored so far. Athletic competition is often and rightly compared to "war with rules" precisely because of their common themes of dominance and destruction.

Notice how this winning-is-everything attitude has corrupted aspects of life as varied as navigating the political process to negotiating the price of a car. Even though we often rail against divisiveness in polite society, our behaviors reveal that we love divisiveness when it's called "sports." Logic thrives on conflict, and an us-versus-them mentality is a logical fear-based construct, not a human one.

The life that the sports metaphor suggests is one in which you're always slugging it out with your "competition" (other humans) from the moment you wake in the morning to the moment you lay your head down at night. In this metaphor, you're constantly on guard for the next assault by those other humans who want to tear you down.

A winning-is-everything approach to competition requires you to dehumanize your opponent first. Think about how you would play a sport differently depending on who your opponents are. For example, if your opponents are family members or close friends, how aggressively would you play to defeat them? Would you ever engage in actions that you even remotely thought could cause injury or pain, temporary or lasting? Or, overtly celebrate your victory in ways that are specifically designed to cause humiliation in your opponents? Yet, those very actions are cheered from the stands and earn competitors the title of "champion."

Our capacity for logic is the only process that supports dehumanization because logic needs an enemy (an opponent) to feel useful. Once you have accepted dehumanizing others as a useful strategy, you will eventually find it useful to treat people in all areas of your life as opponents instead of fellow humans.

That's the reality of being "in the game" of sports, business, and life. Do you really want that to be the theme of your life or that of your children? If that is how you see the world, your children will honor that by being just like you. Asking and answering those questions for yourself is part of the responsibility of being a parent.

So, realize how different the goal of humanity is from that of competition. Parenting, and life in general, asks us to treat others, not just friends and family, as honored lives, first and foremost simply because they are fellow humans. Imagine a world where that is what we model for our children. And, in that world, athletic competition will be viewed far differently than it now is.

The Tale of the Trophy

A high quality of life is its own inspiration because that life cares about creating the best possible outcomes, and because it is also the way to contribute the most to your fellow humans and the world we all share. Tearing others down so that you can "feel like a winner" is counter to creating a high quality of life.

There is no personal version of success separate and distinct from an optimal internal experience, and nothing destroys your internal experience faster or more completely than pitting yourself against other humans. Once again, this is our opportunity to peel back the veneer of the societal paradigm in which althetic competition has been given a seal of nobility that *shall not* be questioned, and instead take an honest look at the very real side effects of this attitude.

Logic's fascination with conflict rises to the surface in many ways, some easily recognizable, others not so. There's a controversy in youth athletic circles about whether to award youth sports trophies just to those who actually win in competition or to all kids who participate in sports (dubbed "participation awards").

The argument for limiting trophies to the actual winners is obvious and a universal practice in adult sports. But the argument for participation awards is that kids are different, and that we should acknowledge kids for just showing up and being active.

Another argument says that there are many privileges like socioeconomics and genetics that are often primary factors in determining who ultimately wins in sports, but none of that is within the control of the child. (Those are also real factors in adult sports, but we conveniently choose to ignore them for the sake of the noble storyline.)

You've probably heard this debate before and perhaps even come to your own conclusion about it. In a group conversation at my gym one day, the prevailing attitude was that participation awards were a dumb "communist/hippie" idea that robbed kids of any motivation to compete at their highest level, thereby defeating the whole purpose of sports. It's clear that the dominant attitude is that winning is the only value in sports. A relative few have stepped forward to claim the case for participation awards.

That day in the gym, it occurred to me that I didn't wholly agree with either viewpoint. For me, the question isn't who gets the trophies but why we give kids trophies at all. What is a trophy if not a symbol for dividing us into winners and losers? Is that the message we want our kids to get from sports? Even participation trophies on some level promote the idea that kids who participate in competitive sports are better than those that don't, as evidenced by the trophy.

If you're willing to entertain the thought of not awarding any trophies, then it becomes a short leap to the question, "Why do we encourage our children to compete against one another in the first place?" Is this really the best thing that we can be teaching kids: how to ensure that their friends become losers? Only logic comprehends and sanctions causing someone else to feel bad. Humanity has no use for that.

This is not a stand for abolishing sports for kids or adults. Rather, I suggest we simply ask ourselves if sports should be glorified as they are now through the awarding of trophies and the inevitable recognition (of winners, at least) they produce, or should athletic competition instead be merely tolerated with the understanding that it is not a human's finest hour. In that way, only the truly gifted athletically and those with a passion for the activity itself will be the likely participants. Isn't that how it should be?

When we glorify any attitude, activity, or behavior and regard it as a symbol of some positive life-lesson that we want to promote, especially in our children, shouldn't we be extremely careful to ensure that it is actually what it claims to be, and that the character it promotes is one of humanity and not conflict? Not only do youth sports glorify seeing people as "winners and losers," they also sow the seeds of an us-vs.-them view of the larger world.

Fun and Games

Don't let the word "game" influence your attitude, as in, the "game of football". Youth sports are not games; they are serious competitions meant to pit humans against each other for bragging rights and the entertainment of others. The word *games* is used only to hide the dehumanizing nature of what happens there. These games appeal only to the ego of both the participants and the spectators. Ask yourself, would there be any physical competitions if there were no spectators to cheer them? There is no greater evidence of an ego-driven concept than something that would not even exist without the adoration and aggrandizement of outside observers.

A true game needs no spectators and focuses instead only on the process rather than the end. In other words, it focuses only on the personal challenges that unfold in the process of reaching a finishing point and the creativity used to overcome those obstacles. We already have those, and they're called arts and adventures. Think again how differently sports would be viewed if the opponents were friends and family, and where overt domination would be unthinkable even for the most logic-centric among us.

The word "game" is intended to refer to something that is fun for all parties. The primary difference between games and competition is in how participants feel when they lose. The difference is entirely personal, but it is also evidence of a negative effect on one's spirit.

If losing isn't as satisfying as winning, then perhaps participants lose even in victory. It is a loss of spirit, of humanity. Show up at a youth sports competition sometime and watch the faces of the kids who lose the game. You'll have all you need to see the ego's involvement in what you are observing.

I was in a conversation with a friend who commented that, in his experience as a young competitor, most coaches were quick to help the kids feels better about a loss and put the best possible spin on it that they could. It made me realize that this effort must be acknowledged and that many great youth coaches out there really believe in what they're doing and in helping to make it a great experience for the kids.

I know this friend was trying to present a positive side to youth sports, but he was instead making my point for me: why are youth sports coaches put in the position of having to help kids feel better about a loss? Doesn't that prove that we have set kids up to feel bad about losing in the first place, and that it then requires someone who cares about the experience of it enough to step in and help them feel better? If the kids had never been made to feel bad about losing, there would never be a need for this extra encouragement, laudable though it may be.

The Health Connection

From those who promote athletic competition for children, you'll also hear that playing sports is about health. Kids and adults mostly believe that if we're competing in an athletic contest, we're also getting healthier. It is true that desires of the ego are incentives to work harder than we otherwise would. And to work harder at something physical, an activity that moves us generally in the direction of better conditioning, appears to be a good thing. Except when it isn't.

All the strategies and tricks for achieving a physical advantage over your competition will eventually surface in the pursuit of winning because that's what "winning is everything" means. Many of these strategies, sadly, are a compromise of health. In other words, there's a downside, a side effect, an impact on the individual's overall quality of life in the short term, long term, or both.

The point is that, if we are going to continue to allow the word athlete to imply only a competitive involvement in sports where winning is the dominant (or only) goal, we must acknowledge that it is also code for "willing to sacrifice short- or long-term health for the sake of winning." That's a message our kids will inevitably hear and model, along with the rest of the compelling but distasteful aspects of competition: ego-satisfaction, bragging rights, false nobility, and so on.

The most obvious folly of connecting a winning-is-everything attitude to health is the ailments that emerge as a result of performance-enhancing drugs among pro athletes who dominate their sport. And, those athletes do win. But they also suffer later ccurrences of brain cancer and liver damage, and those are only the most common. So clearly the "everything" in that sentiment includes a sacrifice of health.

The primary reason that P.E.D.s are banned is not that the governing bodies of the various sports are trying to protect the health of the athlete who would otherwise willingly use these substances. Rather, the purpose is to level the playing field by protecting the choice of competitors for whom winning is *not* everything, and does *not* include compromising their overall quality of life and their future for something as trivial as a trophy and a paycheck.

When winning is everything, health-compromising strategies get people measurably closer to that goal. When athleticism that supports Aliveness is the goal, one would never make a life-compromising choice, and competition with other humans is always a life-compromising choice.

The Real Winner

As I mentioned earlier, Aliveness is its own reward. It can be equally motivating to every part of you except the ego because only you will know what you've created and only you will enjoy the benefits. Sorry, no pats on the back, no high fives, no fist bumps, no trophies, no accolades, no podium appearances, and definitely no bragging rights. There is no quality-of-life award to place on the mantle. Just you and a life lived to its full potential.

I understand that the common narrative about those who dominate in sport is that they are the ones who worked the hardest and played the smartest. This is a nice romantic notion that is seldom true and misses the point of success. It is more often true that the genetically gifted can dominate their sport with even a modest commitment to hard work and knowledge.

The original world in which humans evolved supported their instincts and provided everything necessary for a great experience. Sure, ancient times were rough, but it lived up to its promise of providing that which caused their bodies and those of their children to thrive. And they never had to think about it or understand it. Somehow, that isn't good enough for our logical brains that are always seeking something new and improved, believing they know how to do it better.

There is a distinct absence of opportunities for kids (or anyone) to engage in natural activity in our modern and artificial environment. Outdoor, open, and natural spaces where kids used to engage in play and all manner of activity barely exist in today's urban environment. We're lucky if they even have a mature tree to climb. It's easy to see why parents would try to fill that void with sports, which is one of the very few options for activity that still exist in our artificial world.

Sports are also chosen by some because of the common belief in their supposed character-building potential. As we've seen, athletic competition is about dominating other people and forcing them to acknowledge your superiority or submit to your will. That is textbook egotism, which is logically attractive, to be sure, but ego is rarely considered a noble aspect of character. A loftier sign of character would be the ability to spot the contradiction in the perceived nobility of sports and the disreputable nature of the human ego, whether we engage or not.

There are some sports, of course, that are honest enough to cut the subterfuge and get right to the point of literally crippling your opponent. These are sports like boxing, MMA, cage fighting, and others. These are sports wherein the rules allow you to beat the other person into bloody submission or, in some admittedly rare cases, actually end their life as legitimate ways to achieve the goal of winning.

The other difference with these "sports" is that they generally aren't referred to as "games", but the conceptual leap from those that are identified that way is a short one. I'm glad that those sports exist because they give us all a more honest look at what competition between humans is really about, separate and apart from the romanticized narrative. The notion of winners and losers is a classic logical construct.

The more logic-centric among us have no problem believing that someone else must be dissatisfied with their life in order for you to be satisfied with yours. That's the zero-sum, black and white nature of logic. Is this really the best version of humanity? By now, I hope you are able to connect the dots between this glorification of competition and the negative impacts from it on so many aspects of our personal experience and society as a whole.

My only intent here is to invite a questioning on the part of each of us. This questioning is a personal one designed only to ensure that you are fully aware of the issue and all of its ramifications, and are never mislead by the marketing. This is especially valuable for anything that has taken on the specter of nobility. If we buy into societal paradigms of nobility without this questioning, we fall prey to the presumption of all nobility; that is, as something unavailable to be challenged.

Take a fresh look at how we value competitive sports. It is not just a simple matter of whether awards should go to only the winners, or to all participants. For as much as we love to debate that one, we seem blind to what competition is doing to our children on a far deeper level and how it corrupts everything crucial to life, liberty, and the pursuit of happiness.

There is no need to abolish or even outwardly condemn youth or professional sports, and that is not the suggestion. A simple shift in our understanding of it that includes the negative effects will produce its own result and will foster a new equilibrium that serves humanity better.

We have only to look around us to see the effects of competition on life everywhere. The logic-minded can always justify those effects as insignificant and the inevitable byproducts of human nature. Instead, I see them as tragic, unnecessary, and dehumanizing effects, and a misuse of logic that we ourselves encouraged in our children and cheered on from the stands.

This, then, is one—and only one—of the seeds that we plant in our children that is attractive to their burgeoning capacity for logic, and in opposition to the humanity with which they came into this world. Logic will always promote the notion of life as a competition, and of people as opponents and enemies. This perspective contrasts with our humanity in which we view people as those we might otherwise care for and support as we would have them do for us. Not just our teammates, but all other people.

Is competition with others really the best of humanity? Is this what we really want the dominant or even acceptable theme of our culture to be? And more important, are these the values we want to be teaching our children? Unless we can check ourselves and our egotistic desire to "feel like a winner" at the expense of others, we will always pass that on to our children.

I'm happy to present that different reality for you to consider. And I, for one, will be happy to let it take on a life of its own. But recognize that we are all susceptible to seeing the world through the lens of logic, and logic will not endorse this new approach; logic has a firm hold on the old one.

Real life—the one you are experiencing right now—feels and works best when you build other people up to succeed, knowing that everyone's success is really your success, society's success, and humanity's success also.

Humanized winning means we all win or we all lose together. It's about living in peace, never having to look over your shoulder for the next assault, and knowing that your fellow human also wants the best for you, not the worst. That's a much better description of the things that deserve to be considered noble.

EIGHT
Alive Instead

Key Message:
Life is like ice cream. What flavor would you like to enjoy today?

I've devoted a fair number of words so far to challenging the concepts of health, nutrition, fitness, competition, and even science as irrelevant to a quality life. That conclusion may have caused some to question my grasp of reality.

It wouldn't be helpful at all to simply disparage our capacity for logic and all the constructs that spring from it without providing a new choice, a more powerful alternative that, conveniently, is relevant to how we all experience life. There is no value in any advice that doesn't also offer a new choice for every old one that no longer serves you. In this case, the new choice is found in being unreasonable, but in the same way that your favorite flavor of ice cream is unreasonable.

Regardless, my challenges to logic may cause you to believe that I am somehow justifying a passive existence that is destined for underachievement, resignation, inaction, and a shortened lifespan. If you can just refuse to participate in that logical train of thought for a moment, you'll likely see that there are many other potential outcomes of unreasonableness. And all of them have the benefit of life being lived to a greater, not lesser, extent.

Some of that realization will come from recognizing the true meaning of life for a human; that meaning is found in the concept of Aliveness. Aliveness is just a word that describes an intent for your actions, and recognizes some inconvenient truths about us. Such as the fact that humans are unreasonable at their core. We possess the unreasonable capacities for imagination, creation, love, gratitude. These are only inconvenient to our reliance upon logic. We're only inhibited in that regard by our logical striving for reason.

There is a way to sort this out for yourself with a simple test: the test of Aliveness. With that test as your filter, you will become instantly aware of any supposed "fact" about health, fitness, and programmed diets that don't have the quality of your life as a goal. Instantly. Never again will you be persuaded to adopt some "truth" about your life that is really designed only to sell you something.

Here are four of the earmarks for Aliveness. They will also serve nicely as a test for determining the value of health, fitness, or diet information by the standard of Aliveness:

1. The message is void of absolutes.

Words like "healthy" and "fit" and "correct" and "proven" are sure signs that speakers do not know or care about the quality of your life. Rather, they use these words to justify the supposedly absolute value of a product or practice because, after all, that's all they really can do. Aliveness is never an absolute but is a continuum of possibility valuing only the experience of life.

2. The goals are stated as experiential values.

When goals are about Aliveness, they are never stated as a number or anything observable. Those are logical goals. For example, numerical weight loss is presented as a noble and logical goal. But, in terms of Aliveness weight loss is not the number on the scale or a clothing size; weight loss (if that is even what you need) is the absence of weight that limits the capacity for activity that supports one's purpose and experience. That's a crucial distinction.

For example, if you make an arbitrary amount of weight loss your goal, you will have that and nothing more. If you make extraordinary capacity for purposeful activity your goal, you will have appropriate weight loss and a thousand other benefits—including a significant contribution to the world and your own satisfaction with life—that are byproducts of that result.

3. The information or advice acknowledges the quality of your experience.

This is a recognition that the goal of life is larger than the stated goals of health, fitness, and diet and, in some cases, mutually exclusive of them. Aliveness is a life seeking its highest potential and is always characterized by a high level of internal comfort and satisfaction (free of stress), and it features results that are in full accordance with individuals' vision for their own future.

4. Any stated goals and outcomes will contribute to more than just the individual.

Cosmetic values, for instance, contribute only to the individual.

The irony here is that what seemingly contributes only to the individual doesn't even do that! It is only a satisfaction of the individual's ego. If there is any prime directive of Aliveness, it is that fulfillment in life results only from action that also contributes to the world. This is essentially what distinguishes life-affirming action from fear-based (ego-driven) action.

The current societal paradigm on health fails this test on all counts. It is loaded down with messages of absolutes, quantification, and cosmetics. These values are never about how you feel about your life, but rather about some universal and logically justifiable version of success. You have no doubt noticed people in your immediate circle who flit from one health/fitness/diet trend to the next. Each one is greeted with renewed enthusiasm as some new "breakthrough discovery."

Lead or Follow

In my experience running a health club, I noticed my own employees teaching clients new fitness or weight-loss practices they saw, read, or heard about somewhere. They would glom onto these new theories as if they had just discovered the cure for cancer, and there was no end to it.

For all I know, those same people are still uncovering "new miracle breakthroughs" at a clip of about one per week to this very day. Funny that these new and improved theories and practices will be forgotten as quicly as they arrived in favor of the next. That part never seems to change.

We knew how to accomplish the results many "breakthroughs" ago, and we seldom fully practiced what we knew then. It's only logic's craving for "miracle breakthroughs" and "secret knowledge" that drives the constant search for new theories before we even practice the old ones.

From this we know that it was never really about achieving the goal; it was about turning life into a competition. In this version, we get to be in an exclusive club that has the "secret keys" to winning. Once again, that means winning the competition of life.

When life is a personal experience instead of a competition, logic no longer drives the bus. What drives the experience bus is acts of creation. Creation is the process for living life on our own terms and by our own design because the pursuit is based entirely on how that particular creation makes us feel. We will simply never conceive of a creation that feels bad.

Creation starts with using your imagination to conceive of the experience you want to have, regardless of the experience you're currently having or one that logic tells you is likely. We're often so busy trying to rid ourselves of our current experience that we never actually get around to imagining the one we'd like to replace it with.

Do you see how unlikely it is that we'll move away from our current experience and on to something better if we haven't yet intentionally imagined that something better? This includes whatever results we're looking for in the pursuit of health, fitness, and diet.

Logic (along with almost every personal trainer) tells us that discipline is the way to effect change in your health, fitness, diet, and life. But think about what discipline is. Here's one plausible definition: *a rigid process that compels you to follow some predetermined schedule of actions that are assigned to you by an external source*. The acts of discipline are inevitably dictated by a "plan," a "program," or a "formula," which is always just a theory about what makes a better life. This is a process that denies who you are and posits some theory about who you *should be*.

In this way, the modern versions of self-improvement and success are never about you or your life. They are about your need for safety and a substitute for your own innate wisdom which you no longer trust. Unless both the intent and the actions necessary to achieve the result originate with you and you alone, it will not be about your life.

Imagination, not discipline, is the uniquely personal way to create something about your life that doesn't yet exist, including those things we call health, fitness, and body weight. The great thing about creation is that the path to it will never conflict with who you are and the vision you have for your life. In fact, it will always be a path to the realization of just that.

Creative vision needs no justification or rationale, and engaging in it is effortless. This simple action will always produce at least some degree of what you imagined. More likely, the results will far exceed that vision. And it's always greater than what you will achieve by any other means, especially discipline, hard work, and advice from experts. The hardest part of this process is the suspension of a logical view of life. Instead, creative vision is an unreasonable process (and isn't it fun that "unreasonable" is now a constructive choice) and in perfect keeping with how life works.

Creative action can never be forced or manufactured by a response to fear, an act of will, discipline, or any desire for correctness or recognition. Creative action is the spark of life. You can see it in others, and you'll know if and when it's present in your own life. No matter your age, disability, or limitations, that spark of life will find a way to create something brand new and exciting. Humor and vitality are the ultimate test.

The Game of Aliveness

As we discussed earlier, beyond satisfying our need to survive, life is just a game. You play the game by discovering more about yourself and the world and by creating new visions for your life and your future. Anything that excites you qualifies. For that, you'll want to consider what you perceive to be your unique gifts and how exactly you'd like to use them to serve the world. You'll never regret any activity that matches that description.

Creative visions are fluid, of course, and are subject to change often throughout your life. In fact, if your idea of success doesn't change from time to time, it's an indication that you're stuck in a story about your life rather than in your actual life, like the story of being healthy when there is no such thing. Your ability to achieve any version of a created life will be enhanced, and perhaps made possible at all, when you feel a strong emotional connection to it. If we assume that near-term survival at this point won't require much from us, we become free to merely play with the details.

If details are what you're craving right about now, realize that you already know everything you need to know to raise your life to an extraordinary level. To create entirely new results, you need stronger engagement with the possibility of a new experience, not information. Following "rules for life" just makes us the same as everyone else who's following those same rules.

In my own journey I found very little help outside myself because there wasn't any. No one else can fully understand what stimulates more life in me, and even if they did there is no language to support it. This is how I learned that are no rules that are even remotely crucial to the process. For me or for you. Rather, the answers are only found in the discovery of personal truth.

Unknown and Unknowable

How does someone engage in this discovery? It is the

inevitable result of any set of actions that explores what is unique about you instead of what is commonly sanctioned by others. "Commonly sanctioned by others" is just a fancy way of saying that you "care about what others think of you."

One way to look at it is the opposite of what goes on inside a gym or health club. In that environment, the machines and other paraphernalia, along with the earnest personal trainers, are all there to tell you what you *should be* doing. Plus, you will most likely mimic what you see others doing so as not stand out as some weirdo. Those are examples of a sanctioned path.

Discovery is the substance of every adventure, including the one that reveals who you are. An adventure doesn't give you the opportunity to choose all of the circumstances that lead you to the goal. Rather, it is the stimulation you receive from going somewhere new, doing something new, and encountering something unexpected—better yet if there's an element of risk and hardship involved (real or perceived). Only now the adventure happens entirely within yourself.

The risk of personal discovery is that you must become who you discover yourself to be, whatever that is and no matter how different that is from the person you have been. Since there is no sanctioned version of who you are, discovery will always involve choices the impact of which are unknown and unknowable. Therefore, the only trick to this is finding the courage to accept the unfamiliar, the inconvenient, and the uncertain nature of life. Humanity is always a courageous choice.

Human life thrives when we can remain in "discovery mode." In that mode, the ever-changing landscape of our personal reality and emotional response is much like the changing scenery outside the window of a moving train. Moving life forward requires us to accept everything that comes into view equally, welcoming the scenes we didn't choose as enthusiastically as the ones that we did.

Meanwhile, improving on the quality of Aliveness (including the abundance of it) begins when we are able to break with the Conversation about things like the science of health, fitness, and nutrition as being about who we are. To engage in the Conversation about any shared truth is to favor a very homogeneous experience of conformity over possibility. Aliveness is, instead, an exceptional, unique, and personally satisfying result.

Honoring Life

So, the real paradigm of life is only that which honors all of life. A common attitude in modern society is to honor only those lives that have already achieved greatness or something logically useful. This, in fact, fails the test for honoring life. It doesn't recognize the possibility in each of us, already present or not. The act of honoring a life is the act of acknowledging a person's potential for greatness, not just the greatness that has already emerged. It's the difference between being a cause for that greatness and being just an observer of it.

Honoring your own life follows the same principle. When you pursue a life that's merely common, you fail to acknowledge your own uniqueness. If you withhold honor from any life simply because that greatness has yet to emerge or is otherwise unknown to you, you're likely to treat your own life by this standard. As with experiences, all people are equally capable of making massive contributions to the world, whatever their background and age. To honor your life is to become a champion for the potential of your life, regardless of your current circumstances.

Finally, honoring your life is no different from loving

yourself. Loving someone doesn't mean you will accept, support, and defend only that which you understand and agree with; it means accepting, supporting, and defending aspects that you don't understand and that challenge your current beliefs. If no one has ever honored you in that way, you have never been loved. If you haven't honored yourself in that way, maybe you have not loved yourself. Yet.

NINE
A Mild Case of Dead

Key Message:
Like all living beings, humans are unreasonable at their core. Forcing life to conform to reason is a mild case of dead.

A sign of modern times is a sort of numbness we have to our actual and current experience. Our approach to life in these times is one in which our internal experience is assumed to be largely or completely irrelevant in favor of the external image of it and the data about it. That's one symptom of rational thinking. Our brains are designed to calculate a rational way forward, and that way can be absolutely correct while, at the same time, robbing you of your life.

Would it be important for you to lose those 10 pounds if doing so caused you to feel worse? It very well may. Most of us would readily and naturally assume that losing 10 pounds is a profoundly logical and constructive thing to do, but when was the last time you achieved a fitness or health benchmark you had set and never bothered to check if your life was actually better as a result?

I had a stock recommendation for all my fitness clients:

There's great benefit in the experience of being both overweight and underweight at some time in your life. Likewise, great benefits come from the experience of being an accomplished performer (athletically speaking) combined with the experience of being an underperformer at some time in your life. The opposing scenarios should occur as close to each other as possible while the memory of them both is still fresh.

The intent here is to show people how to identify the experiential states known as overweight and underweight in a non-quantifiable, non-judgmental, and non-crowd-sourced way. In other words, I wanted to give them these experiences in a way that matters to only the individual and no one else. After all, individuals are the ones who must wear and experience their weight; no one else can possibly know the weight that is the most desirable. Neither can the bathroom scale.

Not even clinicians (doctors and nutritionists, for example) can precisely identify the ideal weight for anyone. They will convey a statistical range in which most people tend to live the longest and have the fewest diagnosable physical issues, but that is a squishy value that misses so many of the factors that make up an individual's purpose and quality of life. What's missing from this statistical analysis is what happens at the fringes of the range and beyond. Sometimes it's better.

If you value weighing less as desirable, it may surprise you to learn that weighing less to an extreme is no more desirable than weighing more to an extreme. On both ends of that spectrum, your life takes a drastic turn for the worse.

The same can be said for any physical benchmark people routinely work for, like lifting maximum loads or holding a plank for an extended amount of time. At the edges of any performance curve, you'll find those whose lives are less satisfying than the lives of those in the middle. Yet, my gym was full of people whose attitude about every physical benchmark was "more is better." You see this attitude everywhere in the realms of health and fitness, but more is only better for the bragging rights of it. For everything else, just enough is better. Such is life as well.

When more-is-NOT-better new worlds of opportunity open up for the quality of your life. Here are a few principles designed to produce contributions to Aliveness:

Ceasing to be a victim of your physical state -

Since you created each of the conditions (both ends of the bell curve), you will never again be a victim of your current state because you created that too. Opposing states—no matter which you perceive as the more desirable—are equally within your ability to control. It is the feeling of being out of control that drives so much of the knee-jerk desperation that so-called experts can capitalize on. This is especially true in the realm of weight loss.

Acknowledging experience over measurement -

How you felt in all instances will tell you if those extremes—or any points in between—are the better experience. A better experience is all you want to be working for. Anything else is just a theory about specialization that nature will eventually punish.

But you will know this only if you avoid the quantification and commonly accepted benchmarks for success and turn your attention instead to how you feel and how your life is working as a result.

Appreciating personal truth as a value -

There is a very real difference between the experience of

any physical benchmark and the accurate measuring of it. The measuring is a universal truth that is understood by all and that makes you available for judgment. The experience of it is a personal truth that affects only you, and that you are free to control without the need for justification of any kind. You need only be aware of how it is affecting your ability to be a force in the world for the sake of purpose and satisfaction.

The insulation from experience that keeps us seeking clinical values instead of experiential ones is the same mindset that causes us to trade away our current life for a future one, as with the concept of retirement. We'll justify years of sacrificing passion and suffer countless indignities, all rationalized with the noble sounding logic of "paying our dues."

The more we allow this thinking in our lives, the more numb we become to the draw of passion and integrity. The presumption is we're sacrificing for a later life in which all becomes perfect, but the same *perfect* is available to you this day, hour, and moment. There is never a need to sacrifice any of it for some future prize. That prize will be even greater if you don't.

Just as people glorify life in retirement as a noble pursuit, they glorify the quest for physical goals they also perceive as noble. In both cases, there's always regret for the people and experiences that were sacrificed for the sake of it. Those sacrifices may or may not also involve actual injury (physical sacrifices that cause pain and limit function now or later). Trading away any present moment for the sake of a future one experientially is to live with a self-induced condition that can be described only as "a mild case of dead."

A Mild Case of Longevity

Early on in my college education I conducted a survey on

perceptions about the aging process for a sociology class project. I got the idea from reports on recent gains in human longevity that were being described as a breakthrough of science. But the only conclusions drawn were strictly about the duration of life, never the quality of it.

This inability to reduce quality to a number is inevitable because quality is not quantifiable and therefore is hard to convert into data useful in science or in stories about it. I had already observed that the quality of life in our country was declining. From that, I knew quantity and quality had to be two distinct values. For longevity measured only in years to have value, it would have to mean that people wanted to live a longer life, regardless of the quality of that life. I knew that part wasn't true.

To provide some statistical backing for this theory, I decided to bring it down to the individual level with a simple survey. The lone question I asked a random sampling of 100 people was, "Do you want to live to be 100 years old, yes or no?" Before I pass on the results, take a moment to ask yourself how you would answer this question.

In the final tally, a remarkable 73% of respondents answered no, they wouldn't want to live to be 100. It's clear the majority believed it is no longer a matter of how long we *can* live, but how long we *want to* live and do it well. I learned from these responses that a considerable number of us have lost hope in our ability to enjoy life for the duration of our *current* longevity. Enjoyment is a purely internal and uniquely personal experience.

All science, and every logical conclusion, is only theoretical because we don't know what we don't know. All we really know is not the truth, but rather what seems more true than the truth we used to know. That will be different tomorrow, but your life won't wait. The closest we can ever come to the truth about the quality of our lives is what is known as empirical truth; that is, truth based on wisdom, observation, and our current experience.

In modern times, the relevance of empirical truth is being replaced by theoretical truth. This is a symptom of the dominance of logic over experience. Experience is empirical, something we can know for sure because life itself is empirical, and only that. Theory will always remain something "out there" that may be or should be true but is remote, separate, and distinct from our current experience. However, that current experience—the answer to the question "how are you?"—is all we ever need to live our best lives. Empiricism is never debatable because it's simply "what is" about you, whereas science is always what might or should be.

The real and only source of empirical truth is the "you" who lives inside your skin. You won't find it in external circumstances, good genetics, nutritional supplements, intelligent exercise, or any product or body of knowledge. Just you, your amazing ability to be aware, and the abundant world in which we live.

Different Types of Dead

As you might have guessed, a life that relies on logical constructs and that denies the value of raw experience as a guiding force produces some degree of a condition known as dead. We know this because experience is where alive happens, and without it, we will suffer from a certain case of the opposite, in inverse proportion to your satisfaction with your current experience.

But this reality will never be apparent to the individual who believes that the line between dead and alive is determined only by a scientific analysis of data that separates the two; a.k.a., a pulse. Aliveness is a matter of degree determined entirely by the quality of the experience. When this approach to life is embraced and acted upon, we begin to see how much in control of our own lives we really are.

As I wrote this book, I did some research to see who else was talking and writing about our experience of life as a goal unto itself rather than a potential byproduct of pursuing one of the vast number of theories about life. I couldn't find even one of the self-proclaimed experts in the field of health, life sciences, nutrition, personal development, longevity, or fitness who considers experience to be a value in and of itself. Lots of theories about weight loss, performance, aesthetics, and such, but no life.

Yet, we know conclusively that our current paradigm is wholly flawed because of the results it's producing. Those currently living a suboptimal experience aren't the rare exception who suffer from some disadvantage or lack of information that prevents them from knowing the truth. Instead, they are among the majority of earnest people who have simply followed the natural tendency to trust logic for answers about the experience of life; something logic was never designed to address.

Looking for answers outside ourselves is a pursuit for those who won't do the things we already know will give our bodies a more vital and longer life. The failure to act on behalf of our own lives and longevity can be explained only as a passive form of suicide. That is, suicide by neglect. We all have a lot in common with a potential jumper on the ledge. In many ways, the difference between us is just the length of the fall.

What we share is a poor experience of life. The point of life is a deep understanding of why we're alive in the first place, and enjoying the journey to fulfill that purpose. (Hint: Six-pack abs are not a purpose.) Whether or not we choose to focus on the experience of our lives will determine if we live long, vital and fulfilled lives, or just slug it out until some sad and unnecessary end.

Those scenarios may seem entirely disconnected and disparate, but they are, in fact, evidence of the degree to which we are honoring life as opposed to living it correctly. Just doling out more information and science on health and fitness will certainly not help people who queue up at the fast-food drive-through for meal after meal and then head home for an evening in front of the TV. There's nothing about the destructive nature of those choices they don't already know.

In the same way, you'll never talk a jumper off the ledge by reading the results of a scientific study on the causes of suicide or, worse, by sharing a copy of a pamphlet titled The 5 Highly Effective Habits of People Who Do Not Kill Themselves as a reason to live. It's time we quit looking toward a mythical lack of information as the cause of destructive choices.

It's far more valuable to see those choices for what they are: a lack of trust in one's innate and unreasonable wisdom. It's a failure to recognize why it's a great idea to continue living as well and for as long as possible. That is something all of us instinctively know.

There are many experiential crises in the world today, especially, it seems, in Western culture. A few that immediately come to mind are obesity, depression, Type II diabetes, drug and alcohol abuse, Alzheimer's disease, and an accelerated physical decline in later years. However we decide to tackle these issues, we will fail to improve the situation significantly if we don't acknowledge them as a crisis of spirit first. In other words, there is a spiritual component that is missing in the majority of people who experience these issues and that is present in those who don't.

The crisis of spirit is a crisis of the value we give to life as compared to logic. Life of all kinds. What humans have mostly forgotten from earlier times is that life is sacred, wherever and of whatever kind it is. To humans in modern times, life has become just another inconvenient problem with which we must deal, to be controlled and managed for our logical pursuits, however poor the experience produced by that attitude may be.

The root of this degradation in the value of life is found in our overreliance on the process of logic that encourages us to judge life. That process results in finding some of it good (worthy of being allowed to continue) and some of it bad (well, you know...). Logic dictates that this is a perfectly reasonable thing to do, given logic's own standard of correctness and perfection.

But when you allow any life to be subjected to logical analysis, that same mental process will eventually turn on your own life. Everything about your life becomes available for analysis to be judged worthy or unworthy. One thing we know about this process is that it doesn't feel good, and it gets worse the more we pursue it.

Some of the unworthy traits are the very ones that contribute to the quality of your experience and make you unique in all the world. It is those things that will eventually be deemed unworthy because they serve only your experience, which is not the goal of logic. The goals of logic include efficiency, correctness, productivity, and anything quantifiable.

What Is an Experience?

The way to think of experience is this: It is what remains in the absence of judgment. Life used to be honored instead of judged. A physical environment suffering from the decimation of wildlife habitats and entire species is but one casualty of a judgmental attitude toward life of all kinds.

Life that we consider to be expendable has been judged to be irrelevant because our logical minds can't find any justification for it. Humans will one day discover just how relevant all life is and how little logic understands that, which I hope happens before it's too late. But that revelation can begin only when we recognize how relevant our own lives are.

Too many of us are slowly opting out of experience as a source of guidance because we can't logically justify it. It doesn't fit the narrative of *correctness* and *being smart*. If we try to address the many forms this spiritual crisis takes with another new exercise routine, miracle fat-burning formula, or book on the seven steps to financial freedom, we will miss the heart of the matter: what life is all about.

Before the industrial age, we would have never considered opting out of a deeply personal engagement with our lives. For one thing, doing so would quickly prove fatal. In the absence of doctors and other scientists, the internet, dieticians, personal trainers, anti-aging experts, and voluminous readily available opinions, personal engagement in all forms was a requirement for surviving and maximizing the experience and length of life. There was no medical insurance, Social Security, retirement accounts, or other opportunities for us to opt out of life while we were still among the clinically alive.

I'm not suggesting that we look to the Stone Age to find our bliss, but rather to realize so many aspects of our humanness haven't changed since those times, and we therefore have many lessons to learn from the ancients. Once we're willing to acknowledge where we came from and how little the activities of modern life actually contribute to our experience of life, we can move forward to create a vastly superior level of Aliveness.

By today's standards, Aliveness shows up in qualities that are rare even among those who are described as healthy: qualities like vitality, creativity, and longevity. So, let's be sure to take advantage of the lessons we need from a time in history when humans were far more robust in their interaction with the world and never gave up on themselves and their ability to be self-sufficient and fulfilled. Those are the very qualities that have largely disappeared in today's citizens of the world.

However, we also need to acknowledge some very significant influences at work against this goal. Creating a thriving life sounds a lot like another item for your to-do list. In other words, it seems like something to find a way to avoid. Although there's always a way to avoid it, it will appear very different once your reality has shifted from universal to personal. Once you connect emotionally to the benefits of engagement, the actions you take will become effortless and natural and never feel like a chore. For people who struggle with finding motivation to go to the gym or eat right, this connection ought to be something very exciting to look forward to.

We already accomplish much in our lives without feeling as if it's a burden on our resources or a chore of any kind. One example is packing our bags and getting to the airport for a tropical vacation. From the moment we book our travel to the moment we arrive at our ocean-front villa, we're required to perform many practical, and sometimes difficult, chores such as buying new clothes, packing suitcases, notifying the post office to hold the mail, tucking away travel cash and the passport, getting to the airport, and getting from the airport to the villa. I'll bet, though, that none of it feels much like a chore.

The difference between those tasks and the tasks that you'll find a way to avoid is a personal connection to the goal. That's the experience of it. The energy we spend naturally in preparing for a vacation is produced by the personal connection we have to the experience of being on vacation. Specifically, we have a strong desire to experience what awaits us at our destination.

The thought of relaxing by the pool, cocktail in hand, laughing with a companion, and softly flipping the pages of a great book produces an emotional response. That's pretty much the point of it. And in that emotional connection, all perceptions of effort or burden about the tasks that were necessary to get there disappear. We perceive actions to be a burden or take any note of the various costs involved only when we don't fully comprehend the value of the goal on an emotional level or when there just isn't any.

Life Is An Emotion

So, the new game plan is to seek out an emotional response to our activities that will remove any sense of obligation or self-sacrifice from the actions required because actions are definitely required. You can still force yourself to take action with no emotional connection; this is often referred to as willpower or discipline. Discipline is the productized version of passion. No one can make money from *your* personal experience of passion, only from *their* strategies for discipline.

But without any emotion attached to it, action alone misses the point of your life. An emotional connection changes action from being just another chore to being an exciting part of what you're creating. The lack of an emotional connection is usually the sign that this action is not contributing to the best version of your life.

Likewise, willpower is just one of several emotionless calls to action that fall under the category of motivation. Whenever the failure to accomplish something is blamed on a lack of motivation, it's evidence that we had no emotional involvement in the goal. Nobody ever missed a flight to Hawaii due to a lack of motivation.

We all have an emotional connection to an outcome that we perceive as gratifying. The intent here is not to dictate to you what your own personal gratifications should be, but rather to free you up to become aware of those yourself. We're all capable of creating a much broader range of desirable results than we currently enjoy, and these results expand into far more areas of our lives than we thought possible.

The predictable outcomes of the practices known as health, fitness, and weight loss that are relevant to the greater quality of life are all available to you by way of simpler constructs. What is absent from these goals is anything unique to you. Logic is a shared truth, about commonly understood and agreed-upon conclusions. That means it never produces an answer or solution that is about you; it is always about whatever is common among us and universally valued.

In universality, there is certainty, but no life. When we turn our attention to other approaches that also involve the experiences of life that are unique to each of us rather than to a universal truth, we touch so many more areas of life, and ones that actually improve our current experience.

An example of an experience that is unique to you is what you want. You know what you want only by virtue of an experience, a thought that creates a pleasurable response in you. That is the defining characteristic of wanting. When you stand in front of the freezer case at the grocery store considering all the flavors of ice cream available there, what process do you use to choose?

A flavor of ice cream is a choice that is unique to each of us, evidenced by the fact that someone standing near you and working on the same question will arrive at an entirely different answer. There is always an answer, and no answer is right or wrong. Neither does this choice ever require any data or justification. It is undeniably illogical.

Yet, I've known those who will try to turn a simple choice into a problem that demands a correct answer. Because "correct" is a judgment, it requires data to analyze and calculations to make. In that process, the only *correct* answer is the flavor of ice cream that was chosen by a majority of other people like you in the past. That would occur to your logical brain as an entirely rational choice, but it is instead a decision that has nothing to do with you, which is no choice at all.

Life is like ice cream. What flavor would you like to enjoy today?

A Life of Discovery

When you approach life with logical constructs like health, fitness, and diet, the result can be only a justifiably "correct" one that has nothing to do with you. By just shifting your process to one that includes the experience of what you want (also known as emotion and passion) as the primary consideration, you end up with a completely different outcome that serves a purpose that is unique to you but not limited to you. There is nothing correct or justifiable about it, and there is no need for there to be. The result is always one of satisfaction.

What this approach does require is a process that includes your willingness to discover rather than decide who you are. Discovery is never rational or deliberate; it is merely observing what is for the first time. Discovery is the only learning that children engage in from infancy to the time they're taught to talk and read. They never question whether the lesson is correct or acceptable.

Discovery continues to play a crucial role in life through adolescence. This is the learning that happens as a result of simply being engaged in life. This shift happens when they just pay attention to the immediate environment and have a sincere desire to understand it for the sheer joy of the experience, free from any expectation or obligation. All of this is just an acknowledgement of DNA-level wisdom about how the world works.

Remembering, once again, that the goal here is to live a life to its full potential and free of regret, it is important to cast out everything that does not serve that goal. No one else can ever dictate to you what that looks like or how to achieve it. Only you know, and you know only because you allow experience (how you feel in the moment) to inform your choices. What feels better is always the better choice.

Also, life is not a clinical matter, like health, fitness, and weight loss. Life does not end only when a clinical professional says so. It is not determined by your pulse, brain activity, or anything measurable. It can and does end when you no longer feel the undeniable satisfaction of being alive and when your presence ceases to be a contribution to the world. That is the beginning and the end of the life you were meant to live.

You were all of that on the day you were born. It is only what has happened since that determines your current state of

Aliveness, and everything that has happened since can always be undone. But this is where you must take over and explore the possibilities of who you once were and still are, never refusing to challenge anything and everything that doesn't bring you closer to Aliveness.

Devoting yourself to clinic matters is a distraction from this path, not a way to it. Whatever fails to contribute to your experience and your contribution to the world keeps you mired in something less: a mild case of dead.

TEN

A Bigger Life

Key Message:
Aliveness is the only human performance that equates to the satisfaction of life, the only fitness and health that matter.

I wrote this book to encourage anyone who wants to enjoy life more to consider making the human condition called *alive* the new focus of your energy. To be alive means that all of life can be explained and improved by being more aware of where you are on the continuum of experience from great to less great in each and every moment. A greater quality of life in all ways is a result of honoring the human design instead of the clinical substitutes known as health, fitness, and body weight.

You are not primarily a human, you are primarily a spiritual being. No matter how correct your health and fitness strategies may be, they are not the reason you're here. When you have accomplished absolute control of your body, who is left to care for your spirit.

Beware The Fearful Future

A new fitness platform appeared on the scene recently that promised to train its clients in the style of the most bad-ass military units (you know the ones). This platform's marketing message promises to make you "harder to kill." That promise is representative of the deeper message of the constructs of health, fitness, and diet. It is a message of fear, a belief that there is a force that not only can but also has a mission to end your life.

Too many people who entered my gym had already conjured this fearful world for themselves and were there to do battle with the enemy by training their bodies to be a fighting force. Where is the nobility, not to mention the joy, in a life where threats to safety and prosperity are omnipresent and considered normal?

The normalization of the world as a hostile place rarely reveals itself plainly as it does in this example, but less obvious examples are everywhere in advertising and politics. And they serve as a reminder that many so-called life-enhancing products and practices are promoted on the promise of protecting you from your own perceived fears and a certainty of unseen threats, thereby supporting those notions in you.

This is not a fun way to live, but even worse is the fact that, as long as you are running from imaginary threats, you are also not contributing to the world, the lives of others, the lives of your family, or your own life. This fearful way of life is steeped in judgment and regrets, and will remain essentially unlived. It is a life that has ended in all ways but the clinical one. In other words, it suffers from a mild case of (already) dead.

I can assure you that any great work of art, including a painting, music, or poetry, always enhanced the experience of the artist first, before it was ever released into the world. For artists, the elevation of their own experience is the only source of guidance there is. In their eyes, the creation of art is never considered to be work, a chore, or an act of self-sacrifice; in fact, it is exactly the opposite. Instead, the creation was first and foremost an act of self-love and an expression of humanity.

The default way of humanity is for each of us to live the life of an artist. Our medium is the world and our subject is a fulfilled life. As it is for all artists, a life that contributes to the world is a life of no regrets; we will never regret time spent creating a better experience for ourselves or others. No one regrets actual experiences, only the absence of them. Even the less desirable experiences are called adventures.

Likewise, regret is just another way of saying dissatisfaction, which is the feeling produced by chronic noncontributory effort and busyness. In essence, I'm saying that you cannot separate a contribution to your own experience from one that contributes to the world at large. To be a joyful human is to also be a contributing human. The two are inseparable.

Do health, fitness, and a regimented diet have the potential to contribute in this way? Everything has that potential depending on the intent of the actions taken. In this case, when the intention of our actions is to support a purpose apart from the purely physical, and with the potential to benefit others.

Do we celebrate Christmas only with gifts to ourselves? Have we forgotten that the Christmas spirit is a reminder of how to live a fulfilled life? Even gifts for others are far more meaningful when they are hand-made creations that could have only come from you. They certainly don't need another name or any scientific justification.

The Opposite of Dead

Our obsession with the notions of health, fitness, and weight loss, beyond the scope of Aliveness, is one of noncontributory pursuits. We pursue them for the sake of our ego's desire for safety and recognition. Moving toward any external goal before you are living an internal life that is free from struggle will not result in a legitimate version of success. That better internal life will still feature the occasional intense emotion including sadness, but will also be free from struggle and will realize that purpose and quality of life are one and the same.

What about the goal of longevity? Isn't that a larger purpose?

Longevity is a byproduct of where you are on the continuum of experience. In the end, you will die when you are supposed to. It is how you live in the meantime that matters. However, there is ample evidence that the single-greatest determinant of longevity is not any version of health but a clear and passion-driven purpose. Purpose maximizes the flow of energy through your body, which is a great description of life itself. A life of purpose is a life that wants to live. A life that wants to live knows how to do that better than any health, fitness, or nutrition coach ever will.

But here I need to be clear about the concept of purpose, as I intend it. It's tempting to try to turn purpose into a decision instead of a choice. That is the logical version of purpose. Here's how to not only avoid that trap, but also to get the most of the concept in the context of health:

The non-logical version of purpose is that which results from allowing your life to breathe on its own, without effort, interference, or thought. It is the focus of your passion rather than a creature of your thinking. It is the actions you take and the results you observe that bring personal joy. Another way of saying it is that purpose is the subtext for the actions you take and what gets created purely for the experience of it.

Purpose is never something to be decided upon, nor is it ever realized directly in language. If you are asked what your purpose in life is, it is likely you will be unable to put it into words. Instead, purpose comes from the same place in the human spirit as love, creativity, passion, and wonder and is revealed only when you're not trying to identify it. Also, purpose is never carved in stone; it is likely to change periodically throughout your life and sometimes from morning to afternoon. You will give birth to, and fulfill, many versions of your purpose in your lifetime. Some concurrently.

Your purpose is already at work in you. It is the reason you engage in any action for which you are not being paid or otherwise influenced to do by some external force. If you allowed yourself to pay attention to your actions in those moments without the interference of analysis, you would recognize the purpose behind it. You only truly know purpose in the rear-view mirror, but you can know the process for discovering it right now.

Your best life—your best body—thrives on that kind of purpose and is a creation of it. That kind of life/body cannot be duplicated with contrived health practices. Purpose and creation are both byproducts of living experientially because they are based on what feels best, which also describes thriving itself.

No one would ever think to create something that wasn't personally pleasing to him- or herself first. Likewise, no one would consider a purpose to be something that didn't feel good first. If you can't describe the action as enjoyable, it is also not an act of creation.

Finding enjoyment is just one of the reasons learning to live experientially—being guided by experience instead of rules—is crucial to a thriving life that is both sustainable and unshakeable. The purpose I speak of here is not something you need to go out and find. It is already in you, just waiting for you to stop thinking about it.

A Better Version of Success

In modern times we have become convinced that some version of success is necessary for living a fulfilled life. Remember that "successful" is always a label given to someone by others. When we self-identify with success, we call it happy and grateful. Happy and grateful is also the version of success that humans who lived in historic times enjoyed. The source of this personal success is the same then as now: internal wisdom.

This innate wisdom provides something very different from that which produces envy and recognition. Yet, the more we rely on recognition in the pursuit of a fulfilled life, the more we tend to replace our own wisdom with theory and debate. A reliance on external resources also makes us susceptible to predatory profiteering and misguided, or outright false, information. Unless you're guided by experience, you have no viable benchmark that is about your life.

I'll repeat something here that I said in the Introduction: Don't expect the words written here to be the change. Words can only suggest the change that is possible. The actual change is found in personal exploration and discovery. That is our contribution to the result. Even so, I find myself constantly disappointed in my ability to come up with the right words for the change I'm suggesting. Occasionally, I have to admit that there are none.

Communicating something so profoundly personal in language is a challenge. But this I know: Undertaking any life-enhancing plan because it sounds like it should work is a classic example of logic-based action that consists only of the minutiae of do's and don'ts. When you get to the heart of the actions you take on behalf of your life, you'll also reap the greatest benefit from those actions.

If we miss that shift, we'll just end up with busyness, like every version of exercise. An action with no emotional connection becomes drudgery, another chore on the to-do list, a problem to overcome, a necessary evil, and an onerous obligation. Isn't this the way most of us feel about health practices, a fitness routine, and (definitely) dieting? And, armed with this understanding, it's easy to see why I had to exit my life's work in a field that promoted only discipline and not passion.

All these processes make for a poor outlook on life, and a poor outlook on life and Self always results in a compromised physical state as well. Always. And the opposite is also true. A bright outlook on life will always result in a higher degree of physical wellness. Whether we can clinically support that or not doesn't negate the reality of it. In that way, perhaps it will be recognized that I haven't left the field after all; only changed the words to describe it.

What I have just described is the outcome of Aliveness. Among the qualities of Aliveness that are universal is the experience of moving through life with a certain ease and freedom from fear and internal conflict. Your alignment with that is a great indicator of your understanding of life.

We can't ignore the significance of sex in this discussion. One of our biological imperatives is reproduction. That is valid and not to be dismissed. However, this drive must be brought out into the open and understood to avoid it becoming the ruler of our beliefs and behaviors based on assumptions instead of reality.

As a knee-jerk response to this imperative, it is possible

that we are subconsciously afraid that we won't have any sex unless we achieve some artificial standard of attractiveness. That message—either covertly or overtly—shows up in advertising and casual conversation everywhere. It seems clear this is the belief that drives so much of the cosmetic focus of fitness.

As with so many other misguided notions in the societal paradigm, a closer examination is usually all that is needed for a significant course correction that improves our experience of life. If you are someone who honors your life as a priority you will have all the sex you could possibly want. And, it will be great sex because honoring your life is the surest guarantee that you will attract, and therefore have sex with, others who also care about their life. That is the recipe not only for great sex, but also for great relationships in general; mostly the relationship you have with yourself.

But what are we doing instead? We are dressing up the outside of our bodies with the intent of attracting others to have sex with, but we are still unresolved people inside that cannot contribute to a relationship in any way other than with an attractive body. That attractive body may indeed have a lot of sex, but it will likely be with people who have also dressed up their outside as a maneuver to hide their own internal struggles with life. When we are not resolved ourselves we are far less able to identify resolution in others.

In effect, all this cosmetic fitness is counter to the intent of the biological imperative of reproduction (or, at least, the act that often results in reproduction). Instead of supporting that imperative, health, fitness, and weight loss are the loopholes that allow us to bypass the step of honoring our lives as a means to satisfying that imperative. Once again, without the uncomfortable work of changing who we are on the inside, we seek only that which is apparent to outside casual observers who do not really know our internal experience of life, or perhaps even care. That often includes those who ask, "how are you?"

No Pain, No Gain

People in workout circles pride themselves on their willingness to endure physical discomfort as the path to their goals. We've all heard the line, "no pain, no gain". But the "pain" they're talking about is of the external kind; the purely physical. Those who pride themselves on enduring the physical discomfort of exercise often recoil in horror at the thought changing who they are on the inside. There's an inconsistency in our thinking that can be challenged when and where we find it.

The world and everything in it gets better when we are at peace with who we are on the inside—including the quality and quantity of sex and intimacy with others in general. Only our ego is satisfied by the bragging rights and cosmetics of fitness.

Working to improve one's physical state is always a constructive strategy for a better life in many ways, and I would never discourage fulfilled people from adopting a more active life for any reason. But fulfilled people don't need my encouragement, and gyms and health clubs and jogging trails are full of unhappy and unfulfilled people who are desperate for a distraction from their thoughts and the reality they perceive.

Clinically speaking, mental health and physical health appear to be entirely separate issues, and they're universally referred to separately in the Conversation. But as with so many things that we've identified already, the only value in that separation is a clinical one, for the sake of analyzing or measuring or comparing.

It's also true that mental health and physical health are taught as separate disciplines in institutions of higher education. This is another paradigm we ought to question. Addressing them separately is the equivalent of believing the power in your action is a separate issue from the reason you're taking that action. In the real world—where people experience life, not just talk about it—it's plain that an exceptional degree of Aliveness is always tied to this integrated life.

Likewise, mental outlook and physical robustness are inextricably linked, and each is treated as necessary for the success of the other. There, the emotional energy that powers actions determines the results those actions will produce. Here, too, each is a necessary contributor to optimal results.

The logical brain is so good at gathering data and critical analysis that it not only provides the correct answers, but it will seek out new problems and convince us of their validity and urgency, just for the sake of occupying itself and justifying its analytical (read: fearful) way of seeing the world.

That activity can overwhelm our awareness to the point that we can forget entirely about our spirit, which is always sitting quietly and patiently waiting for us to once again value experience over theory. Is your life dominated by this fearful brain activity? Obsessions with health, fitness, and diet are pretty good clues that the answer is yes.

Choice is a Creation

If we don't consciously make a choice, the brain will steal the entire show of our awareness and become our chronic way of seeing the world. As a result, we appear to be afraid of not being afraid. Some of us will fear spiders, some will fear heights, some will fear flying, and so on, but the real damage occurs when we fear life, the people around us, and our own bodies. There's ample evidence that none of these are real fears; otherwise, we would all be afraid of all of them. They are, instead, just interpretations of what is. Where else does that exist?

The art of life is no different from any art; it is a creation rather than a calculation. You create only when you ignore the data that is a requirement for analysis. Any creation is, by its very definition, something brand new and never before conceived. A work of art is something for which no historical data exists, and which needs no logical justification. There are no facts and figures to describe your life and to tell you whether or not you are correct, you will be appreciated, you are contributing, or you will be loved and respected and admired.

To move forward with your life as a creation instead of as a math problem is to surrender to the fact that it will never be sanctioned by logic. Logic demands data to crunch, measurements to make, people to dominate, and comparisons to make. In the end, though, it is just the act of honoring your experience that tells the story, and that is the only act that will ever produce a life of greatness.

The honoring of your life as a creation requires more in the way of participation from you, in addition to the courage you must bring to the process. You must create. There is no passivity to this life; in fact, it is the polar opposite of passivity…it is the pinnacle of a life in action. Whenever there is a question about how to achieve greater success in health, fitness, or weight loss, the answer is shockingly simple and always the same: Honor your life more.

Imagination means having the courage to speak something into existence, to draw a mental picture that has never before existed and cannot be justified in any rational sense. That is real courage. When we have the courage to elevate who we are through the power of our own imagination, everything in life falls in line to support that vision, both inside and outside ourselves.

When you turn your imagination onto yourself, it will change the very nature of who you are. This requires a significant degree of courage, and logic will not condone it. But to do anything else is to merely settle for the picture that was presented to you as a child. That may have been a good picture that serves you well in most cases and has allowed you a degree of success that, by all appearances, is exceptional. However, it is still lacking one crucial ingredient of life: It isn't your picture.

When analyzing data becomes guidance for your life, you are not only setting yourself up for a mediocre existence, but you are also inviting your past to determine your future. That means that your past becomes more important than it needs to be. If that is a past of dysfunction and trauma, it becomes a corrupter of the future. When your life is a creation of your own making, the past has only the influence that you give it, and it need not have any at all.

I hear so many people say that the way they are, no matter how uncomfortable and ineffective, must be just who they are because they have always been this way. This is often true of those with a lifelong history of being overweight. That is a report on the source and quality of the data they have been using to determine their future, the data of their history.

It is true that you cannot rewrite history, but you can, instead, make that data irrelevant by refusing to participate in the notion that it somehow dictates who you can be today.

Every life lost through misunderstanding is a loss not just to the individual, but also to the world. The poet John Donne first posited this idea way back in 1624 when he penned the words, "No man is an island." From this, we know that embedded in the answer of who we are is also the answer to our purpose and our contribution to the world. We're all left to wonder what the world has lost because of life's simple misunderstandings. But we can always ensure that those misunderstandings don't extend to our own lives.

You Already Know

One of the first signs of a corrupted experience is that we attempt to address our quality of life by breaking it down into its individual parts (like fitness, diet, health, exercise, weight loss, health clubs, personal trainers, and pills) so that we can pick and choose the one we decide to take on first, or ever. This approach never produces much in the way of actual quality of life. Mostly, we never get beyond step 1, if we even fully address that one.

Did you ever wonder why no one has taken a living human body completely apart as you would some mechanical device—an act which would, of course, kill it—with the intent to then put it back together and restore life to it? Because it can't be done. It violates the design of life. This is a metaphor for your experience.

Nevertheless, that is what we try to do every day with that very same body and our quality of life. To deal with the parts of our life individually is folly. All those parts are inextricably connected and affected by each other. They simply cannot live as disconnected parts. They may have an appearance of life, and they may pass some clinical test for life, but there is no "you" in that equation.

While working in the fitness field I met truly sincere people who came into my gym wanting to get or stay active and capable, yet they were sabotaging their lives in several other ways at the same time, effectively negating whatever efforts they could produce in the gym. But they believed that gym time would reverse the damage. In that way, the modern version of fitness—with its fancy health clubs and expensive running shoes—is enabling the dehumanizing effects of our logical lives.

Imagine for a moment that we could ban all indoor activity, and make it illegal to teach theories about life when we also have so many empirical truths about it. We would be left with nothing but our lifestyle, and we would come face-to-face with the destructive nature of it. We could no longer claim that there was a way to compensate for it or that it doesn't matter. This is the shift that I'm suggesting.

An entire industry has been built on allowing you to believe that, if you just hit the gym a few times a week, the result would be good health. Never has this been true, and never will it be true. You can't address the broad spectrum of life with just one little piece of it. That same industry will give lip service to the other contributors to your life's quality, but they have never figured out a way to make money from them, so their roles go largely unaddressed in any meaningful way.

We have very few models for the completeness of life in the trappings of modern civilization. Achieving an extraordinary level of Aliveness will inevitably require changes to your lifestyle that defy the current paradigm. I've suggested those changes often enough in my private coaching practice to realize that they're commonly met with some resistance. This is precisely why they're so rare. If you also feel resistance, keep in mind that your unfamiliarity with it and a lack of societal sanctioning is the source of that resistance.

Most educators on the subject of health make a case entirely dependent on compelling "new information". The premise here is that new information is the missing piece people need to finally do the right thing for themselves. I have said nothing new in this book. My criteria for everything here is things we once knew but forgot.

I reject the notion that people don't know enough to maximize their lives in all of the ways that we can affect. Most teachers and coaches and thought leaders believe that making such a statement would diminish their authority on the subject. The only problem with that belief is that they actually think they have any authority.

Buying into the notion that you are uninformed will lead you to consult educators who are trying to out-science each other. They are often basing the validity and effectiveness of their information on the number of times they use the word *science*. Better still is if they win the contest to see how many other multisyllabic "sciency" words they can sprinkle into their presentations. None of this has anything to do with you.

That singular strategy is the reason billions of dollars are handed over each year to educators whose only purpose is convincing you they hold the keys to your future, and by consumers who desperately want to believe that too. And, because new and "secret" information will finally resolve all of their internal suffering.

To our capacity for logic, being wrong is a fatal flaw. So is not knowing. So is basing anything on how you feel. So is acting without scientific justification. So is laughing out loud. So is falling in love.

It is true that there is plenty we don't know, and much of it is in the process of being looked at by science, but I contend that is the last 1% of physical development, not the place to start. The place to start requires no science whatsoever. In fact, science doesn't even care about the stuff that humans have always known, whether they practice it or not. The personal failing for most of us is that we are doing but a fraction of what we already know.

The ultimate mission of experience is to continuously upgrade our interpretations of reality until we perceive all of it as an enthusiastic opportunity. No truism, recommendations, advice, suggestion, clinical analysis, expert opinion, or 5-Step-Plan can help other people unless it provides them with a new choice that they didn't have, or didn't know they had, before.

Take Back Your Life

Life—human life, your life—is lived to its fullest capacity when it is free from the fear of being wrong. This is counterintuitive only to the brain, but you already live much of your life by this principle, just not enough of it. Freeing our lives from logical constructs, which are any forms of guidance that require numbers, the domination of others, or recognition by others, is the first and only step toward a life of no regrets and a life lived to its fullest.

There needs to be some part of our lives that isn't a competition, a part that is only about the experience of it and that isn't a reasonable choice, like a spontaneous and solo walk on the beach. For that to happen, we must acknowledge the value of life as a goal unto itself. If we validate only that which is logical, we will pursue only that. Life is not logical, as evidenced by the fact that no one can explain why we're all here. Let's learn to honor that part of life.

Is there still a question in your mind about what you should do instead of fitness, health, and nutrition? Are you even a little disappointed that I didn't provide more do's and don'ts of the body? Any request for that is always met with the same response from me: *you already know what to do.* The only thing keeping you from what you already know is asking it to pass the test of logic. The dominant message of logic is always: "You don't yet have enough information to take action." Is logic the source of all procrastination?

Just reading this book means you will forevermore ask different questions and do different things for the sake of your own satisfaction with life. I can't tell you what those different things are because they will be about you, not me. But I can tell you that those things are all that has ever been missing from your life.

As children, we are mostly taught to think, not to feel. Parents who know only how to think cannot teach anything but that. This book is asking you to get back in touch with your feelings, primarily because they are a source of wisdom about the whole of life for which there is no substitute. Thinking is always a response to logic and fear.

Relying on logic for guidance—sometimes referred to as being *in your head* instead of your heart—is always a symptom of subconscious fear. And fear wants you to force an outcome rather than allow it as a result of your lifestyle. Health, fitness, and diet are all concepts designed to force an outcome, but allowing the outcome is still available to you. The difference is that the outcomes you allow are always a matter of degree, not an arbitrary absolute, and those outcomes support only an experience, not a number on a medical chart or recognition from others.

"Alive" is not a clinical designation based on the presence of a heartbeat. It is, rather, a quality of this thing called life. Life defies quantification, a reduction to clinical values, or commonly held benchmarks.

While writing this book, I devoted so much time to it that it caused a compromise in my normal level of activity along with the quality of my nutrition. While I lost some muscle and put on a little body fat in the process, I also never felt more alive. This book was part of my purpose, and purpose is the real engine of life; not health, not fitness, not diet, not money...just passionate purpose.

Whatever physical degeneration has occurred as a result of producing this book, it was both totally worth it and ultimately reversible. I know beyond any doubt that this book was meant to be, and I wasn't about to let some artificial commitment to my "fitness" keep me from this act of creation. Loving your life is the new health.

If you are obsessing about the image your body presents or some aspect of human performance remember that the body is not an end unto itself as we have been made to believe by sports and fitness coaches. Rather, the body is here in support of a purpose. In your life, what is your body supporting? How capable your body is of powerfully and reliably contributing to the lives of others is all you need to know about your physical state. If it fails that test then you are just surviving. Just surviving is not a fun place to be. It is, instead, the model for a mild case of dead.

The New Game

Far too many of us are using our health, fitness, and diet as convenient scapegoats for a poor experience of life. When we can't identify the actual cause of our suffering we will commonly experience it as physical symptoms like stress, incapacity, and other discomforts. If we believe that physical symptoms require physical remedies, we will often look to health, fitness, and diet strategies. No one can argue with the reasoning in that, but if this book is about anything it is about learning to live an unreasonable life.

Remember the part where I said Aliveness is nothing more than eliminating the notions that get in the way of it? Health, fitness, and diet rules are some of those notions. Aliveness, then, becomes the automatic outcome for someone with the courage to stop buying what health is selling—a productized version of life, and start living the personal one.

You may have already figured out that being good at the game of checkers is a metaphor for being good at health, fitness, and weight loss, and the experiential attitude about that is the same: "Wow! You must not be good at very many things." Instead, make your intent to live a generalized and broad-based life, along with the whole experience of it. This is a better experience than being a master of something.

Beyond the egoic logic of it all, what is the end of the pursuit of checkers, health, fitness, and nutritional perfection? For example, what happens when age becomes the dominant factor in others' perception of you and your physical standing? What then?

What happens then is exactly what could have happened all along. Then, you will only retain that which serves your personal fulfillment and supports the activities of life. You no longer care about image or comparison or secret information or physical dominance or superior knowledge. All of those things will eventually fall away, and you will be left with the only persistent factors that are important to life: being supremely satisfied with who you are.

That is the human design. When you get there, you will no longer have any questions because the questions were all about seeking something other than that design. You will finally realize that you already knew what to do all along. You will finally realize that to be settled in your soul is so much more valuable than receiving all the recognition and personal-bests and trophies your body was able to acquire.

Aliveness is the only human performance that equates to the satisfaction of life, the only fitness and health that matter. There are no bragging rights, no winners and losers. Just participants, participating fully in life. Just vitality, quality of life, and living as long as you're supposed to. There are no expectations of being the winner of anything, just the best human you can be. And make no mistake, that is a rare human indeed. To never be the best is also to be exceptional in nearly every way. But those qualities are acquired as a byproduct of a life well lived; they are never the goal.

Choose to be competitive if it lights you up. There is no crime in that if you know what you're signing up for. It comes with a price. Don't assume that appearances equate to quality of life. And, if you're someone who believes that being competitive is the only thing that would motivate a person to be active at all, there's a whole other world I'd like to introduce you to.

In Other Words...

I hope the message you have received here is that it is always noble to take care of your body—always. But never more than you are taking care of your life as a whole, and never with an intention of anything other than perfectly supporting the reason you're here. Following this path may require a wholesale change in the way you conduct your life or require no change at all. You are the one to determine that.

My hope for you is that you find the courage to take back your health, take back your fitness, take back your weight, take back your eating, and make these things about you, not someone else. Since there is no standard for any of them anyway, you get to say what is and is not perfect for your life. No one else can or will tell you what creates the best possible experience of your life. That is the essence of Aliveness.

People take illicit and destructive drugs for the same reason that they obsess about their heath, fitness, and nutrition: they are seeking external answers to internal questions, universal truths instead of personal ones. When you take back the definition of health that works for you in both realms, the world will look completely different than it does today. You will see it through the eyes of the human spirit instead of the lens of logic.

I am so thankful to all the people throughout history who have committed themselves to a purpose when it required obvious sacrifices in their ability to seek recognition and envy from others. Those experience-seekers left gifts for me and for you in the form of music, stories, humor, art, architecture, and companionship.

Purpose is found only in the *you* that is separate from your blood, organs, and muscle and bones. This is the place of the human spirit. It is the part of you that doesn't change as a result of any type or degree of health, fitness, or diet. The human spirit, and the purpose it reveals, will always be the biggest influence on your feelings about your life and an experience that no purely physical change can match.

A life of purpose is an end unto itself. If you choose to pursue anything called health, fitness, or weight loss separately from the reason you're here, those pursuits (by whatever name you call them) are transient and will fade with time. All logical constructs have a short shelf life, and the clock is ticking.

Conversely, purpose and the legacy it leaves are your own creation, and they remain always because of that. There is never any version of "correct" that can produce a life of greatness, nor can "incorrect" ever take it away. Any formula-for-a-better-life that consists only of science, shared truth, and clinical values, regardless of the subject, will only result in the condition forever more known as a mild case of dead.

The proper function of man is to live, not to exist. I shall not waste my days in trying to prolong them. I shall use my time to live.

- Jack London

www.ingramcontent.com/pod-product-compliance
Lightning Source LLC
Chambersburg PA
CBHW020420010526
44118CB00010B/349